From a photograph by Chandler, Philadelphia

Edward W. Bok

A DUTCH BOY
FIFTY YEARS AFTER

BY

EDWARD BOK

ADAPTED FROM
"THE AMERICANIZATION OF EDWARD BOK"

EDITED WITH AN INTRODUCTION BY
JOHN LOUIS HANEY, Ph.D.
PRESIDENT CENTRAL HIGH SCHOOL, PHILADELPHIA

CHARLES SCRIBNER'S SONS
NEW YORK   CHICAGO   BOSTON
ATLANTA   SAN FRANCISCO

TO

**THE SCHOOLBOYS AND SCHOOLGIRLS
OF AMERICA**

I DEDICATE THIS STORY OF A BOY
WHO BELIEVED THAT AN OBSTACLE IS NOT SOMETHING
TO BE AFRAID OF
BUT IS ONLY A DIFFICULTY TO BE OVERCOME
AND WHO TOOK FOR HIS MOTTO
AS I HOPE EVERY ONE WHO READS THESE PAGES WILL DO
THESE LINES BY MADELINE S. BRIDGES:

*" Give to the world the best you have
And the best will come back to you."*

Edward W. Bok

INTRODUCTION

In recent years American literature has been enriched by certain autobiographies of men and women who had been born abroad, but who had been brought to this country, where they grew up as loyal citizens of our great nation. Such assimilated Americans had to face not only the usual conditions confronting a stranger in a strange land, but had to develop within themselves the noble conception of Americanism that was later to become for them a flaming gospel. Andrew Carnegie, the canny Scotch lad who began as a cotton weaver's assistant, became a steel magnate and an eminent constructive philanthropist. Jacob Riis, the ambitious Dane, told in *The Making of an American* the story of his rise to prominence as a social and civic worker in New York. Mary Antin, who was brought from a Russian ghetto at the age of thirteen, gave us in *The Promised Land* a most impressive interpretation of America's significance to the foreign-born. The very title of her book was a flash of inspiration.

To this group of notable autobiographies belongs *The Americanization of Edward Bok*, which received, from Columbia University, the Joseph Pulitzer Prize of one thousand dollars as "the best American biography teaching patriotic and unselfish service to the Nation and at the same time illustrating an eminent example." The judges who framed that decision could not have stated more aptly the scope and value of the book. It is the story of an unusual education, a conspicuous achievement, and an ideal now in course of realization.

At the age of six Edward Bok was brought to America by his parents, who had met with financial reverses in their native country of the Netherlands. He spent six years in the public schools of Brooklyn, but even while getting the rudiments of a formal education he had to work during his spare hours to bring home a few more dollars to aid his needy family. His first job was cleaning the show-window of a small bakery for fifty cents a week. At twelve he became an office boy in the Western Union Telegraph Company; at nineteen he was a stenographer; at twenty-six he became editor of *The Ladies' Home Journal*, which during the thirty years of his supervision achieved the remarkable circulation of two million copies and reached every month an audience of perhaps ten million persons. Such is the bare outline of a career that has the essential characteristics of struggle and achievement, of intimate contact with eminent men and women, and, most interesting of all, is not a fulfilled career, but a life still in the making.

The significance of *The Americanization of Edward Bok* is threefold and is clearly indicated by the author's own conception of the three periods that should constitute a well-rounded life. These he characterizes as education, achievement, and service for others. Conceived in this ideal spirit, the autobiography has a message for every American schoolboy or schoolgirl who is looking forward to the years of achievement and who should be made to understand that there is a finer duty beyond. It has an equally important message for those of us who in the turmoil of a busy world are struggling to achieve, in many instances with no vision beyond the desire to provide as best we can for the welfare of ourselves and our families. Lastly, it has an inspiring, constructive message for those who are now in a position to render altruistic service and thus contribute their share toward making the world in general and America in particular a better place in which to live.

Because of the recognized value of Edward Bok's life-story, the present abridged edition, which is re-named *A Dutch Boy Fifty Years After*, has been undertaken. The chapters here brought together, with the approval of Mr. Bok, tell the story of the Dutch boy in the American school, his earnest efforts to help his parents, his journalistic and literary experiences, his wide-spread influence as editor, and a vision of what he still hopes to accomplish for the land of his adoption.

Our boys and girls who become familiar with the story of this resourceful Dutch lad should note that he is not ashamed to tell us he helped his mother by building the fire, preparing the breakfast, and washing the dishes before he went to school, and when he returned from school he did not play but swept, scrubbed, and washed more dishes after the evening meal. He did not whine and mope because his parents could no longer keep the retinue of servants to which they had been accustomed in the Netherlands. He simply pitched in and helped. The same spirit impelled him to clean the baker's windows for fifty cents a week, to deliver a newspaper over a regular route, to sell ice water on the Coney Island horse-cars—in short, to do any honorable work to overcome the burden of poverty. Meanwhile he strove to acquire what little education he could, but he probably learned more from his association with the prominent persons whom he met as a result of his early passion for autograph collecting. Such a boyhood brings home the important truth that necessity is the mother of self-reliance.

Mr. Bok's story indicates the road to success and gives encouragement to those who would tread that pleasant way, but it also sounds a frank warning against the pitfalls that beset ambitious youth. When he was sent by the city editor of the *Brooklyn Eagle* to review a theatrical performance and decided to write his review without going to the theatre, he had, of course, no warning that the performance would not take place. He took what many a more experienced reporter would consider a reasonable chance and he suffered keen humiliation when the lesson was forced home that it does not pay to attempt deception. He tells us that the incident left a lasting impression and he felt grateful because it happened so early in life that he could take the experience to heart and profit by it. With equal candor he tells of the stock-market "tips" that resulted from his intimacy with Jay Gould. Wisely he records that he resolved to keep out of Wall Street thereafter, in spite of his initial success in speculation. When he gave up an association that probably would have led to his becoming a stock-broker, and somewhat later, when he declined an offer to be the business manager for a popular American actress, Edward Bok was called upon to make fateful decisions. In this story he lays ample stress upon the need for careful and deliberate consideration at such crucial moments.

The account of his long and successful editorship of *The Ladies' Home Journal* reveals the extent of his influence on American social and domestic conditions. He broadened the scope of *The Journal* until it touched the life of the nation at many points. The earlier women's magazines had devoted most attention to fashions, needlework, and cookery, printing a few sentimental stories and poems to give the necessary literary atmosphere. *The Ladies' Home Journal* took up a great variety of problems concerning the American home and those who dwelled therein. A corps of editors was assembled to conduct departments and to answer questions either by mail or in the pages of *The Journal*. Free scholarships in colleges and in musical conservatories were given in place of the usual magazine premiums. Series of articles were published to foster our national appreciation for better architecture, better furniture, better pictures—in brief, for better homes in every respect.

Mr. Bok discouraged the taking of patent medicines, the wearing of aigrettes, the use of the public drinking-cup, the disfiguring of American scenery with glaring signs and bill-posting, the use of fireworks on the Fourth of July, and many similar matters that were not to our credit or advantage. He printed convincing photographs taken in various "dirty cities" that tolerated refuse and other evidences of untidiness on their streets and literally shamed those communities into cleaning up the plague-spots. Had he been a commonplace editor with his main thought on the subscription list he would have avoided controversy by confining his leading articles to subjects unlikely to offend any one, but he would not pursue any policy that meant a surrender of his ideals. When occasion demanded he did not hesitate to hit squarely from the shoulder. Whether the public agreed with him or not, it knew that *The Journal* was very much in earnest whenever it espoused any cause.

Mr. Bok's last important service as editor of *The Journal* was a direct outcome of our participation in the Great War. The problems raised by that world cataclysm called for a restatement of American ideals and aspirations. He therefore arranged for a number of articles adapted to the needs of every community, whether large or small, and these were soon acclaimed as the most comprehensive exposition of practical Americanization that had yet been published.

As a far-sighted editor with a long experience behind him
he knew that many of the immigrants coming to this country were ready to enjoy our privileges without undertaking
to share our responsibilities. The newcomer could realize
a freedom unknown in Europe, he had a chance to achieve
higher standards of living and to establish a better home
for himself and his family; what were we asking in return?
We did not subject him to a political confession of faith
and we did not fix his social caste; were we justified in asking him to accept our language and to uphold our institutions? The intelligent immigrant knows that the culture
of America is a transplanted European culture, but he
quickly realizes that it has become something distinctive
because it developed under conditions where social barriers
or racial jealousies are of slight importance. The person
who grasps this truth, as did Edward Bok, knows well that
America stands ready to accept any man, whether native-
born or alien, at his true worth and will give him unequalled
opportunity to make the most of his abilities.

In accomplishing his Americanization, Mr. Bok learned
much from us and he has given his fellow-Americans a
chance to learn something from him. He is aware of our
pride in what we have achieved, but he points the way to
still greater triumphs in the years to come. He urges us
to give more regard to thrift, to be more painstaking and
thorough in what we do, and finally, to overcome our preva-
lent lack of respect for authority. Such advice is especially
appropriate at this time. During the present critical
period in the wake of the greatest and most destructive
of all wars, a prudent nation will follow the fundamental
political and economic virtues. It is no time for extrava-
gance, for slipshod service, or for defiance of established
law. Our young people need every incentive to make the

most of their talents and of their opportunities. If they observe closely the successive steps of Mr. Bok's career they will understand why he did not continue to wash shop-windows all his life or why the Western Union's office-boy did not grow up to be a mere clerk or local manager. In the important chapters entitled "The Chances for Success" and "What I Owe to America" they will learn that ambition and industry must be supplemented by other admirable qualities in the loyal American who is eager to serve his country to the utmost.

The concluding chapters of the autobiography have a most valuable lesson for every American, young or old. In them Mr. Bok calls upon us to give a helping hand to the other fellow and to accept in more genuine spirit the gospel of the brotherhood of man. The civic pride that urged him to join in the movement to beautify his home community of Merion and that caused his activity in the raising of an endowment fund of almost two million dollars for the Philadelphia Orchestra is what we would expect of the idealist who sets out to observe the wise precept of his Dutch grandparents: "Make you the world a bit more beautiful and better because you have been in it."

Throughout the book the observant reader will note the author's pride in his Dutch ancestry and his consciousness of the fact that he owes so much to the splendid qualities of his forbears. Such pride may be shared by every other progressive American of foreign birth or parentage who feels that he is bringing into our social and industrial life certain commendable traits that characterize the best sons and daughters of his fatherland, whatever that fatherland may be.

The admirable dedication that Mr. Bok has prepared for this little volume is addressed to American schoolboys and schoolgirls, but its message is just as vital for the older reader. In the prime of life and on the threshold of his Third Period, Mr. Bok has begun to give practical demonstration of the kind of service that is possible for those who are sincerely ready to serve. He is alive to the fact that as a nation we are still young and eager to learn. We have made serious mistakes in the past and our institutions are as yet far from perfect, but with more of our intellectual leaders accepting the watchword of altruistic service in the spirit of Mr. Bok's conception, there can be virtually no limitations to the part that America seems destined to play in the future.

JOHN L. HANEY

CENTRAL HIGH SCHOOL
PHILADELPHIA

CONTENTS

ILLUSTRATIONS

AN INTRODUCTION OF TWO PERSONS

IN WHOSE LIVES ARE FOUND THE SOURCE AND MAINSPRING
OF SOME OF THE EFFORTS OF THE AUTHOR OF THIS BOOK
IN HIS LATER YEARS

*Along an island in the North Sea, five miles from the
Dutch coast, stretches a dangerous ledge of rocks that has
proved the graveyard of many a vessel sailing that turbulent
sea. On this island once lived a group of men who, as each
vessel was wrecked, looted the vessel and murdered those of the
crew who reached shore. The government of the Netherlands
decided to exterminate the island pirates, and for the job King
William selected a young lawyer at The Hague.*

*"I want you to clean up that island," was the royal order.
It was a formidable job for a young man of twenty-odd years.
By royal proclamation he was made mayor of the island,
and within a year, a court of law being established, the young
attorney was appointed judge; and in that dual capacity he
"cleaned up" the island.*

*The young man now decided to settle on the island, and
began to look around for a home. It was a grim place, barren
of tree or living green of any kind; it was as if a man had been
exiled to Siberia. Still, argued the young mayor, an ugly
place is ugly only because it is not beautiful. And beautiful
he determined this island should be.*

*One day the young mayor-judge called together his council.
"We must have trees," he said; "we can make this island a
spot of beauty if we will!" But the practical seafaring men
demurred; the little money they had was needed for matters
far more urgent than trees.*

"*Very well,*" *was the mayor's decision—and little they guessed what the words were destined to mean—*"*I will do it myself.*" *And that year he planted one hundred trees, the first the island had ever seen.*

"*Too cold,*" *said the islanders;* "*the severe north winds and storms will kill them all.*"

"*Then I will plant more,*" *said the unperturbed mayor. And for the fifty years that he lived on the island he did so. He planted trees each year; and, moreover, he had deeded to the island government land which he turned into public squares and parks, and where each spring he set out shrubs and plants.*

Moistened by the salt mist the trees did not wither, but grew prodigiously. In all that expanse of turbulent sea—and only those who have seen the North Sea in a storm know how turbulent it can be—there had not been a foot of ground on which the birds, storm-driven across the water-waste, could rest in their flight. Hundreds of dead birds often covered the surface of the sea. Then one day the trees had grown tall enough to look over the sea, and, spent and driven, the first birds came and rested in their leafy shelter. And others came and found protection, and gave their gratitude vent in song. Within a few years so many birds had discovered the trees in in this new island home that they attracted the attention not only of the native islanders but also of the people on the shore five miles distant, and the island became famous as the home of the rarest and most beautiful birds. So grateful were the birds for their resting-place that they chose one end of the island as a special spot for the laying of their eggs and the raising of their young, and they fairly peopled it. It was not long before ornithologists from various parts of the world came to "Egg-land," as the farthermost point of the island came to be known, to see the marvellous sight, not of thousands but of hundreds of thousands of bird-eggs.

A pair of storm-driven nightingales had now found the island and mated there; their wonderful notes thrilled even the souls of the natives; and as dusk fell upon the seabound strip of land the women and children would come to "the square" and listen to the evening notes of the birds of golden song. The two nightingales soon grew into a colony, and within a few years so rich was the island in its nightingales that over to the Dutch coast and throughout the land and into other countries spread the fame of "The Island of Nightingales."

Meantime, the young mayor-judge, grown to manhood, had kept on planting trees each year, setting out his shrubbery and plants, until their verdure now beautifully shaded the quaint, narrow lanes, and transformed into wooded roads what once had been only barren wastes. Artists began to hear of the place and brought their canvases, and on the walls of hundreds of homes throughout the world hang to-day bits of the beautiful lanes and wooded spots of "The Island of Nightingales." The American artist, William M. Chase, took his pupils there almost annually. "In all the world to-day," he declared to his students, as they exclaimed at the natural cool restfulness of the island, "there is no more beautiful place."

The trees are now majestic in their height of forty or more feet, for it is nearly a hundred years since the young attorney went to the island and planted the first tree; to-day the church-yard where he lies is a bower of cool green, with the trees that he planted dropping their moisture on the lichen-covered stone on his grave.

This much did one man do. But he did more.

After he had been on the barren island two years he went to the mainland one day, and brought back with him a bride. It was a bleak place for a bridal home, but the young wife had the qualities of the husband. "While you raise your trees," she said, "I will raise our children." And within a score of years the young bride sent thirteen happy-faced, well-brought-up children over that island, and there was reared a home such as is given to few. Said a man who subsequently married a daughter of that home: "It was such a home that once you had been in it you felt you must be of it, and that if you couldn't marry one of the daughters you would have been glad to have married the cook."

One day when the children had grown to man's and woman's estate the mother called them all together and said to them, "I want to tell you the story of your father and of this island," and she told them the simple story that is written here.

"And now," she said, "as you go out into the world I want each of you to take with you the spirit of your father's work, and each, in your own way and place, to do as he has done: make you the world a bit more beautiful and better because you have been in it. That is your mother's message to you."

The first son to leave the island home went with a band of hardy men to South Africa, where they settled and became known as "the Boers." Tirelessly they worked at the colony until towns and cities sprang up and a new nation came into being: The Transvaal Republic. The son became secretary of state of the new country, and to-day the United States of South Africa bears tribute, in part, to the mother's message to "make the world a bit more beautiful and better."

The second son left home for the Dutch mainland, where he took charge of a small parish; and when he had finished his work he was mourned by king and peasant as one of the leading clergymen of his time and people.

A third son, scorning his own safety, plunged into the boiling surf on one of those nights of terror so common to that coast, rescued a half-dead sailor, carried him to his father's house, and brought him back to a life of usefulness that gave the world a record of imperishable value.   For the half-drowned sailor was Heinrich Schliemann, the famous explorer of the dead cities of Troy.

The first daughter now left the island nest; to her inspiration her husband owed, at his life's close, a shelf of works in philosophy which to-day are among the standard books of their class.

The second daughter worked beside her husband until she brought him to be regarded as one of the ablest preachers of his land, speaking for more than forty years the message of man's betterment.

To another son it was given to sit wisely in the councils of his land; another followed the footsteps of his father.   Another daughter, refusing marriage for duty, ministered unto and made a home for one whose eyes could see not.

So they went out into the world, the girls and boys of that island home, each carrying the story of their father's simple but beautiful work and the remembrance of their mother's message.   Not one from that home but did well his or her work in the world; some greater, some smaller, but each left behind the traces of a life well spent.

And, as all good work is immortal, so to-day all over the world goes on the influence of this one man and one woman, whose life on that little Dutch island changed its barren rocks to a bower of verdure, a home for the birds and the song of the nightingale.   The grandchildren have gone to the four corners of the globe, and are now the generation of workers— some in the far East Indies; others in Africa; still others in our own land of America.   But each has tried, according to the talents given, to carry out the message of that day, to tell the story of the grandfather's work; just as it is told here by the author of this book, who, in the efforts of his later years, *has tried to carry out, so far as opportunity has come to him, the message of his grandmother:*

"Make you the world a bit more beautiful and better because you have been in it."

EDWARD W. BOK

MERION
PENNSYLVANIA
1920

A DUTCH BOY FIFTY YEARS AFTER

CHAPTER I

THE FIRST DAYS IN AMERICA

The leviathan of the Atlantic Ocean, in 1870, was *The Queen*, and when she was warped into her dock on September 20 of that year, she discharged, among her passengers, a family of four from the Netherlands who were to make an experiment of Americanization.

The father, a man bearing one of the most respected names in the Netherlands, had acquired wealth and position for himself; unwise investments, however, had swept away his fortune, and in preference to a new start in his own land, he had decided to make the new beginning in the United States, where a favorite brother-in-law had gone several years before. But that, never a simple matter for a man who has reached forty-two, is particularly difficult for a foreigner in a strange land. This fact he and his wife were to find out. The wife, also carefully reared, had been accustomed to a scale of living which she had now to abandon. Her Americanization experiment was to compel her, for the first time in her life, to become a housekeeper without domestic help. There were two boys: the elder, William, was eight and a half years of age; the younger, in nineteen days from his landing-date, was to celebrate his seventh birthday.

This younger boy was Edward William Bok. He had,

1

according to the Dutch custom, two other names, but he had decided to leave those in the Netherlands. And the American public was, in later years, to omit for him the "William."

Edward's first six days in the United States were spent in New York, and then he was taken to Brooklyn, where he was destined to live for nearly twenty years.

Thanks to the linguistic sense inherent in the Dutch, and to an educational system that compels the study of languages, English was already familiar to the father and mother. But to the two sons, who had barely learned the beginnings of their native tongue, the English language was as a closed book. It seemed a cruel decision of the father to put his two boys into a public-school in Brooklyn, but he argued that if they were to become Americans, the sooner they became part of the life of the country and learned its language for themselves, the better. And so, without the ability to make known the slightest want or to understand a single word, the morning after their removal to Brooklyn, the two boys were taken by their father to a public-school.

The American public-school teacher was less well equipped in those days than she is to-day to meet the needs of two Dutch boys who could not understand a word she said, and who could only wonder what it was all about. The brothers did not even have the comfort of each other's company, for, graded by age, they were placed in separate classes.

Nor was the American boy of 1870 a whit less cruel than is the American boy of 1920; and he was none the less loath to show that cruelty. This trait was evident at the first recess of the first day at school. At the dismissal, the brothers naturally sought each other, only to find themselves surrounded by a group of tormentors who were delighted to have such promising objects for their fun. And of this opportunity they made the most. There was no form of petty cruelty boys' minds could devise that was not inflicted upon the two helpless strangers. Edward seemed to look particularly inviting, and nicknaming him "Dutchy" they devoted themselves at each noon recess and after school to inflicting their cruelties upon him.

Louis XIV may have been right when he said that "every new language requires a new soul," but Edward Bok knew that while spoken languages might differ, there is one language understood by boys the world over. And with this language Edward decided to do some experimenting. After a few days at school, he cast his eyes over the group of his tormentors, picked out one who seemed to him the ringleader, and before the boy was aware of what had happened, Edward Bok was in the full swing of his first real experiment with Americanization. Of course the American boy retaliated. But the boy from the Netherlands had not been born and brought up in the muscle-building air of the Dutch dikes for nothing, and after a few moments he found himself looking down on his tormentor and into the eyes of a crowd of very respectful boys and giggling girls, who readily made a passageway for his brother and himself when they indicated a desire to leave the schoolyard and go home.

Edward now felt that his Americanization had begun; but, always believing that a thing begun must be carried to a finish, he took, or gave—it depends upon the point of view—two or three more lessons in this particular phase of Americanization before he convinced these American schoolboys that it might be best for them to call a halt upon further excursions in torment.

At the best, they were difficult days at school for a boy

of seven who could not speak English.   Although the other children stopped teasing Edward, they did not try to make the way easier for him.   America is essentially a land of fair play, but it is not fair play for American boys and girls to take advantage of a foreign child's unfamiliarity with the language or our customs to annoy that child or to place difficulties in his way.   When a foreign pupil with little knowledge of the English language enters an American school the native-born boys and girls in that school can accomplish a useful service in Americanization by helping the newcomer, thus giving him a true idea of American fairness at the start.   No doubt many American boys and girls gladly do this little kindness for the young foreigner, but Edward Bok and his brother suffered tortures at the hands of those who should have helped them.

Fortunately the linguistic gift inherent in the Dutch race came to Edward's rescue in his attempt to master the English language.   He soon noted many points of similarity between English and his native tongue; by changing a vowel here and there he could make a familiar Dutch word into a correct English word.   As both languages had developed from the old Frisian tongue, the conquest of English did not prove as difficult as he had expected.   At all events, he set out to master it.

Edward was now confronted by a three-cornered problem.   Like all healthy boys of his age he was fond of play and eager to join the boys of his neighborhood in their pastimes after school hours.   He also wanted to help his mother, which meant the washing of dishes, cleaning the rooms in which the family then lived, and running various errands for the needed household supplies.   Then, too, he was not progressing as rapidly as he wished with his school studies, and he felt that he ought to do everything in his

EDWARD BOK AT THE AGE OF SIX
Upon his arrival in the United States

power to take advantage of his opportunity to get an education.

Methodically he worked out a plan which made it possible to accomplish all three objects. He planned that on one afternoon he should go directly home from school to help his mother, and as soon as he had finished the necessary chores that would make her life easier he would be free to go out and play for the rest of that afternoon. On the following day he would remain in school for an extra hour after the class had been dismissed and would get the teacher's help on any lessons that were not clear to him. When that task had been accomplished he would still have part of that afternoon left for play. He broached his plan for work at home and study at school on alternate afternoons to his mother and his teacher. Both approved of the idea and agreed that it had been well thought out.

Thus Edward Bok learned early in life the valuable lesson of a wise management of time. Instead of attempting to accomplish various results in some haphazard fashion, he planned to do only one thing at a time, yet his plan was so comprehensive that it provided for the necessary housework, study, and play—the three things that he wanted to do and felt he should do.

As his evenings were also devoted to various tasks and duties, this young American-to-be, by using each bit of spare time for some useful purpose, became early in life the busy person that he has remained to the present day. Of Edward Bok it may truly be said that he began to work, and to work hard, almost from the day he set foot on American soil. He has since realized that this is not the best thing for a young boy, who should have liberal time for play in his life. Of course, Edward made the most of the short period that remained each afternoon after his household duties or his extra studies at school, and when he played it was with the same vim and energy with which he worked. He had little choice in the matter, but he often regrets to-day that he did not have more time in his boyhood for play.

Like most boys, Edward wanted a little money now and then for spending, but his mother was not always able to spare the pennies that he desired. So he had to fall back on his own resources to earn small sums by running errands for neighbors and in other ways familiar to boys of his age. One day he came across an Italian who was earning money in a rather unusual way. This Italian would collect the bright-colored pictures that adorned the labels of fruit and vegetable cans. He would paste these pictures into a scrap-book and sell it to a mother as a picture-book for her children. Edward saw that the Italian's idea smacked of originality and he asked the man where he got his pictures.

"From the cans I find on lots and in ash-barrels," was the reply.

"If you had more pictures, you could make more books and so earn more money, couldn't you?" asked Edward, as an idea struck him.

"Yes," answered the Italian.

"How much will you give me if I bring you a hundred pictures?" asked Edward.

"A cent apiece," said the Italian.

"All right," agreed Edward.

The boy went to work at once, and in three days he had collected the first hundred pictures, gave them to the Italian, and received his first dollar.

"Now," said Edward, as he had visions of larger returns from his efforts, "your books have pictures of only four or five kinds, like apples, pears, tomatoes, and green peas.

How much will you give me for pictures of special fruit which you haven't got, like apricots, green-gages, and pine-apples?"

"Two cents each," replied the Italian.

"No," bargained Edward. "They're much harder to find than the others. I'll get you some for three cents each."

"All right," said the vender, realizing that the boy was stating the case correctly.

Edward had calculated that if he would search the vacant lots in back of the homes of the well-to-do, where the servants followed the tidy habit of throwing cans and refuse over the back fences, he would find an assortment of canned-fruit labels different from those used by persons of moderate means. He made a visit to those places and found the less familiar pictures just as he thought he would. Thus he was not only able to sell his labels to the Italian for three cents instead of a cent apiece, but to give greater variety to the vender's scrap-books.

In this manner Edward Bok learned to make the most of his opportunities even during his earliest years in America.

CHAPTER II

THE FIRST JOB: FIFTY CENTS A WEEK

The elder Bok did not find his "lines cast in pleasant places" in the United States. He found himself, professionally, unable to adjust the methods of his own land and of a lifetime to those of a new country. As a result the fortunes of the transplanted family did not flourish, and Edward soon saw his mother physically failing under burdens to which her nature was not accustomed nor her hands trained. Then he and his brother decided to relieve their mother in the housework by rising early in the morning, building the fire, preparing breakfast, and washing the dishes before they went to school. After school they gave up their play hours, and swept and scrubbed, and helped their mother to prepare the evening meal and wash the dishes afterward. It was a curious coincidence that it should fall upon Edward thus to get a first-hand knowledge of woman's housework which was to stand him in such practical stead in later years.

It was not easy for the parents to see their boys thus forced to do work which only a short while before had been done by a retinue of servants. And the capstone of humiliation seemed to be when Edward and his brother, after having for several mornings found no kindling wood or coal to build the fire, decided to go out of evenings with a basket and pick up what wood they could find in neighboring lots, and the bits of coal spilled from the coal-bin of the grocery-store, or left on the curbs before houses where coal had been delivered. The mother remonstrated with the boys, although in her heart she knew that the necessity was upon them. But Edward had been started upon his Americanization career, and answered: "This is America, where one can do anything if it is honest. So long as we don't steal the wood or coal, why shouldn't we get it?" And, turning away, the saddened mother said nothing.

But while the doing of these homely chores was very effective in relieving the untrained and tired mother, it added little to the family income. Edward looked about and decided that the time had come for him, young as he was, to begin some sort of wage-earning. But how and where? The answer he found one afternoon when standing before the shop-window of a baker in the neighborhood. The owner of the bakery, who had just placed in the window a series of trays filled with buns, tarts, and pies, came outside to look at the display. He found the hungry boy wistfully regarding the tempting-looking wares.

"Look pretty good, don't they?" asked the baker.

"They would," answered the Dutch boy with his national passion for cleanliness, "if your window were clean."

"That's so, too," mused the baker. "Perhaps you'll clean it."

"I will," was the laconic reply. And Edward Bok, there and then, got his first job. He went in, found a stepladder, and put so much Dutch energy into the cleaning of the large show-window that the baker immediately arranged with him to clean it every Tuesday and Friday afternoon after school. The salary was to be fifty cents per week!

But one day, after he had finished cleaning the window, and the baker was busy in the rear of the store, a customer came in, and Edward ventured to wait on her. Dexterously he wrapped up for another the fragrant currant-buns for which his young soul—and stomach—so hungered! The baker watched him, saw how quickly and smilingly he served the customer, and offered Edward an extra dollar per week if he would come in afternoons and sell behind the counter. He immediately entered into the bargain with the understanding that, in addition to his salary of a dollar and a half per week, he should each afternoon carry home from the good things unsold a moderate something as a present to his mother. The baker agreed, and Edward promised to come each afternoon except Saturday.

"Want to play ball, hey?" said the baker.

"Yes, I want to play ball," replied the boy, but he was not reserving his Saturday afternoons for games, although, boy-like, that might be his preference.

Edward now took on for each Saturday morning—when, of course, there was no school—the delivery route of a weekly paper called the *South Brooklyn Advocate*. He had offered to deliver the entire neighborhood edition of the paper for one dollar, thus increasing his earning capacity to two dollars and a half per week.

Transportation, in those days in Brooklyn, was by horse-cars, and the car-line on Smith Street nearest Edward's home ran to Coney Island. Just around the corner where Edward lived the cars stopped to water the horses on their long haul. The boy noticed that the men jumped from the open cars in summer, ran into the cigar-store before which the watering-trough was placed, and got a drink of water from the ice-cooler placed near the door. But that was not so easily possible for the women and the children, who were forced to take the long ride without a drink. It was this that he had in mind when he reserved his Saturday afternoon to "play ball."

Here was an opening, and Edward decided to fill it. He bought a shining new pail, screwed three hooks on the edge from which he hung three clean shimmering glasses, and one Saturday afternoon when a car stopped the boy leaped on, tactfully asked the conductor if he did not want a drink, and then proceeded to sell his water, cooled with ice, at a cent a glass to the passengers. A little experience showed that he exhausted a pail with every two cars, and each pail netted him thirty cents. Of course Sunday was a most profitable day; and after going to Sunday-school in the morning, he did a further Sabbath service for the rest of the day by refreshing tired mothers and thirsty children on the Coney Island cars—at a penny a glass!

But the profit of six dollars which Edward was now reaping in his newly found "bonanza" on Saturday and Sunday afternoons became apparent to other boys, and one Saturday the young ice-water boy found that he had a competitor; then two and soon three. Edward immediately met the challenge; he squeezed half a dozen lemons into each pail of water, added some sugar, tripled his charge, and continued his monopoly by selling "Lemonade, three cents a glass." Soon more passengers were asking for lemonade than for plain drinking-water!

One evening Edward went to a party of young people, and his latent journalistic sense whispered to him that his young hostess might like to see her social affair in print. He went home, wrote up the party, being careful to include the name of every boy and girl present, and next morning took the account to the city editor of the *Brooklyn Eagle*, with the sage observation that every name mentioned in that paragraph represented a buyer of the paper, who would like to see his or her name in print, and that if the editor had enough of these reports he might very advantageously strengthen the circulation of *The Eagle*. The editor was not slow to see the point, and offered Edward three dollars

a column for such reports. On his way home, Edward calculated how many parties he would have to attend a week
to furnish a column, and decided that he would organize a
corps of private reporters himself. Forthwith, he saw
every girl and boy he knew, got each to promise to write
for him an account of each party he or she attended or gave,
and laid great stress on a full recital of names. Within a
few weeks, Edward was turning in to *The Eagle* from two
to three columns a week; his pay was raised to four dollars
a column; the editor was pleased in having started a department that no other paper carried, and the "among
those present" at the parties all bought the paper and were
immensely gratified to see their names.

So everybody was happy, and Edward Bok, as a full-
fledged reporter, had begun his journalistic career.

It is curious how deeply embedded in his nature, even
in his earliest years, was the inclination toward the publishing business. The word "curious" is used here because
Edward is the first journalist in the Bok family in all the
centuries through which it extends in Dutch history. On
his father's side, there was a succession of jurists. On the
mother's side, not a journalist is visible.

Edward attended the Sunday-school of the Carroll Park
Methodist Episcopal Church, in Brooklyn, of which a Mr.
Elkins was superintendent. One day he learned that Mr.
Elkins was associated with the publishing house of Harper
and Brothers. Edward had heard his father speak of
Harper's Weekly and of the great part it had played in the
Civil War; his father also brought home an occasional copy
of *Harper's Weekly* and of *Harper's Magazine*. He had
seen *Harper's Young People;* the name of Harper and
Brothers was on some of his school-books; and he pictured
in his mind how wonderful it must be for a man to be

associated with publishers of periodicals that other people read, and books that other folks studied. The Sunday-school superintendent henceforth became a figure of importance in Edward's eyes; many a morning the boy hastened from home long before the hour for school, and seated himself on the steps of the Elkins house under the pretext of waiting for Mr. Elkins's son to go to school, but really for the secret purpose of seeing Mr. Elkins set forth to engage in the momentous business of making books and periodicals. Edward would look after the superintendent's form until it was lost to view; then, with a sigh, he would go to school, forgetting all about the Elkins boy whom he had told the father he had come to call for!

But what with helping his mother, tending the baker's shop in after-school hours, serving his paper route, plying his street-car trade, and acting as social reporter, it soon became evident to Edward that he had not much time to prepare his school lessons. By a supreme effort, he managed to hold his own in his class, but no more. Instinctively, he felt that he was not getting all that he might from his educational opportunities, yet the need for him to add to the family income was, if anything, becoming greater. The idea of leaving school was broached to his mother, but she rebelled. She told the boy that he was earning something now and helping much. Perhaps the tide with the father would turn and he would find the place to which his unquestioned talents entitled him. Finally the father did. He associated himself with the Western Union Telegraph Company as translator, a position for which his easy command of languages admirably fitted him. Thus, for a time, the strain upon the family exchequer was lessened.

But the American spirit of initiative had entered deep

into the soul of Edward Bok. The brother had left school a year before, and found a place as messenger in a lawyer's office; and when one evening Edward heard his father say that the office boy in his department had left, he asked that he be allowed to leave school, apply for the open position, and get the rest of his education in the great world itself. It was not easy for the parents to see the younger son leave school at so early an age, but the earnestness of the boy prevailed.

And so, at the age of twelve, Edward Bok left school, and on Monday, August 7, 1876, he became office boy in the electricians' department of the Western Union Telegraph Company at six dollars and twenty-five cents per week.

And, as such things will fall out in this curiously strange world, it happened that as Edward drew up his chair for the first time to his desk to begin his work on that Monday morning, there had been born in Boston, exactly twelve hours before, a girl-baby who was destined to become his wife. Thus at the earliest possible moment after her birth, Edward Bok started to work for her!

CHAPTER III

With school-days ended, the question of self-education
became an absorbing thought with Edward Bok. He had
mastered a schoolboy's English, but six years of public-
school education was hardly a basis on which to build the
work of a lifetime. He saw each day in his duties as office
boy some of the foremost men of the time. It was the
period of William H. Vanderbilt's ascendancy in Western
Union control; and the railroad millionnaire and his com-
panions were objects of great interest to the young office
boy. Alexander Graham Bell and Thomas A. Edison were
also constant visitors to the department. He knew that
some of these men, too, had been deprived of the advantage of collegiate training, and yet they had risen to the
top. But how? The boy decided to read about these
men and others, and find out. He could not, however, afford the separate biographies, so he went to the libraries
to find a compendium that would authoritatively tell him
of all successful men. He found it in Appleton's *Encyclopædia*, and, determining to have only the best, he saved
his luncheon money, walked instead of riding the five miles
to his Brooklyn home, and, after a period of saving, had
his reward in the first purchase from his own earnings: a
set of the *Encyclopædia*. He now read about all the successful men, and was encouraged to find that in many cases
their beginnings had been as modest as his own, and their
opportunities of education as limited.

One day it occurred to him to test the accuracy of the

biographies he was reading.   James A. Garfield was then
spoken of for the presidency; Edward wondered whether it
was true that the man who was likely to be President of the
United States had once been a boy on the tow-path, and
with a simple directness characteristic of his Dutch training, wrote to General Garfield, asking whether the boyhood
episode was true, and explaining why he asked. Of course
any public man, no matter how large his correspondence, is
pleased to receive an earnest letter from an information-
seeking boy.   General Garfield answered warmly and fully.
Edward showed the letter to his father, who told the boy
that it was valuable and he should keep it.   This was a
new idea.   He followed it further: if one such letter was
valuable, how much more valuable would be a hundred!
If General Garfield answered him, would not other famous
men?   Why not begin a collection of autograph letters?
Everybody collected something.

Edward had collected postage-stamps, and the hobby
had, incidentally, helped him wonderfully in his study of
geography.   Why should not autograph letters from famous
persons be of equal service in his struggle for self-education?   Not simple autographs—they were meaningless; but
actual letters which might tell him something useful.   It
never occurred to the boy that these men might not answer
him.

So he took his *Encyclopædia*—its trustworthiness now
established in his mind by General Garfield's letter—and
began to study the lives of successful men and women.
Then, with boyish frankness, he wrote on some mooted
question in one famous person's life; he asked about the
date of some important event in another's, not given in the
Encyclopædia; or he asked one man why he did this or why
some other man did that.

Most interesting were, of course, the replies. Thus General Grant sketched on an improvised map the exact spot where General Lee surrendered to him; Longfellow told him how he came to write "Excelsior"; Whittier told the story of "The Barefoot Boy"; Tennyson wrote out a stanza or two of "The Brook," upon condition that Edward would not again use the word "awful," which the poet said "is slang for 'very,'" and "I hate slang."

One day the boy received a letter from the Confederate general, Jubal A. Early, giving the real reason why he burned Chambersburg. A friend visiting Edward's father, happening to see the letter, recognized in it a hitherto-missing bit of history, and suggested that it be published in the *New York Tribune*. The letter attracted wide attention and provoked national discussion.

This suggested to the editor of *The Tribune* that Edward might have other equally interesting letters; so he despatched a reporter to the boy's home. This reporter was Ripley Hitchcock, who afterward became literary adviser for the Appletons and Harpers. Of course Hitchcock at once saw a "story" in the boy's letters, and within a few days *The Tribune* appeared with a long article on its principal news page giving an account of the Brooklyn boy's remarkable letters and how he had secured them. The *Brooklyn Eagle* quickly followed with a request for an interview; the *Boston Globe* followed suit; the *Philadelphia Public Ledger* sent its New York correspondent; and before Edward was aware of it, newspapers in different parts of the country were writing about "the well-known Brooklyn autograph collector."

Edward Bok was quick to see the value of the publicity which had so suddenly come to him. He received letters from other autograph collectors all over the country who

sought to "exchange" with him. References began to
creep into letters from famous persons to whom he had
written, saying they had read about his wonderful collection and were proud to be included in it. George W.
Childs, of Philadelphia, himself the possessor of probably
one of the finest collections of autograph letters in the
country, asked Edward to come to Philadelphia and bring
his collection with him—which he did, on the following
Sunday, and brought it back greatly enriched.

Several of the writers felt an interest in a boy who
frankly told them that he wanted to educate himself, and
asked Edward to come and see them. Accordingly, when
they lived in New York or Brooklyn, or came to these cities
on a visit, he was quick to avail himself of their invitations.
He began to note each day in the newspapers the "distinguished arrivals" at the New York hotels; and when any
one with whom he had corresponded arrived, Edward
would, after business hours, go up-town, pay his respects,
and thank him in person for his letters. No person was too
high for Edward's boyish approach; President Garfield,
General Grant, General Sherman, President Hayes—all
were called upon, and all received the boy graciously and
were interested in the problem of his self-education. It
was a veritable case of making friends on every hand;
friends who were to be of the greatest help and value to the
boy in his after-years, although he had no conception of it
at the time.

The Fifth Avenue Hotel, in those days the stopping-
place of the majority of the famous men and women visiting New York, represented to the young boy who came to
see these celebrities the very pinnacle of opulence. Often
while waiting to be received by some dignitary, he wondered how one could acquire enough means to live at a

place of such luxury. The main dining-room, to the boy's mind, was an object of special interest. He would purposely sneak up-stairs and sit on one of the soft sofas in the foyer simply to see the well-dressed diners go in and come out. Edward would speculate on whether the time would ever come when he could dine in that wonderful room just once!

One evening he called, after the close of business, upon General and Mrs. Grant, whom he had met before, and who had expressed a desire to see his collection. It can readily be imagined what a red-letter day it made in the boy's life to have General Grant say: "It might be better for us all to go down to dinner first and see the collection afterward." Edward had purposely killed time between five and seven o'clock, thinking that the general's dinner-hour, like his own, was at six. He had allowed an hour for the general to eat his dinner, only to find that he was still to begin it. The boy could hardly believe his ears, and unable to find his voice, he failed to apologize for his modest suit or his general after-business appearance.

As in a dream he went down in the elevator with his host and hostess, and when the party of three faced toward the dining-room entrance, so familiar to the boy, he felt as if his legs must give way under him. There have since been other red-letter days in Edward Bok's life, but the moment that still stands out pre-eminent is that when two colored head waiters at the dining-room entrance, whom he had so often watched, bowed low and escorted the party to their table. At last he was in that sumptuous dining-hall. The entire room took on the picture of one great eye, and that eye centred on the party of three—as, in fact, it naturally would. But Edward felt that the eye was on him, wondering why he should be there.

What he ate and what he said he does not recall. General Grant, not a voluble talker himself, gently drew the boy out, and Mrs. Grant seconded him, until toward the close of the dinner he heard himself talking. He remembers that he heard his voice, but what that voice said is all dim to him. One act stamped itself on his mind. The dinner ended with a wonderful dish of nuts and raisins, and just before the party rose from the table Mrs. Grant asked the waiter to bring her a paper bag. Into this she emptied the entire dish, and at the close of the evening she gave it to Edward "to eat on the way home." It was a wonderful evening, afterward up-stairs, General Grant smoking the inevitable cigar, and telling stories as he read the letters of different celebrities. Over those of Confederate generals he grew reminiscent; and when he came to a letter from General Sherman, Edward remembers that he chuckled audibly, reread it, and then turning to Mrs. Grant, said: "Julia, listen to this from Sherman. Not bad." The letter he read was this:

DEAR MR. BOK:—

I prefer not to make scraps of sentimental writing. When I write anything I want it to be real and connected in form, as, for instance, in your quotation from Lord Lytton's play of "Richelieu," "The pen is mightier than the sword." Lord Lytton would never have put his signature to so naked a sentiment. Surely I will not.

In the text there was a prefix or qualification:

> Beneath the rule of men entirely great
> The pen is mightier than the sword.

Now, this world does not often present the condition of facts herein described. Men entirely great are very rare indeed, and even Washington, who approached greatness as near as any mortal, found good use for the sword and the pen, each in its proper sphere.

You and I have seen the day when a great and good man ruled this country (Lincoln) who wielded a powerful and prolific pen, and yet had to call to his assistance a million of flaming swords.

No, I cannot subscribe to your sentiment, "The pen is mightier than the sword," which you ask me to write, because it is not true.

Rather, in the providence of God, there is a time for all things; a time when the sword may cut the Gordian knot, and set free the principles of right and justice, bound up in the meshes of hatred, revenge, and tyranny, that the pens of mighty men like Clay, Webster, Crittenden, and Lincoln were unable to disentangle.   Wishing you all success, I am, with respect, your friend,
                                                W. T. SHERMAN.

Mrs. Grant had asked Edward to send her a photograph of himself, and after one had been taken, the boy took it to the Fifth Avenue Hotel, intending to ask the clerk to send it to her room.   Instead, he met General and Mrs. Grant just coming from the elevator, going out to dinner.   The boy told them his errand, and said he would have the photograph sent up-stairs.

"I am so sorry we are just going out to dinner," said Mrs. Grant, "for the general had some excellent photographs just taken of himself, and he signed one for you, and put it aside, intending to send it to you when yours came."   Then, turning to the general, she said: "Ulysses, send up for it.   We have a few moments."

"I'll go and get it.   I know just where it is," returned the general.   "Let me have yours," he said, turning to Edward.   "I am glad to exchange photographs with you, boy."

To Edward's surprise, when the general returned he

brought with him, not a duplicate of the small *carte-de-visite* size which he had given the general—all that he could afford—but a large, full cabinet size.

"They make 'em too big," said the general, as he handed it to Edward.

But the boy didn't think so!

That evening was one that the boy was long to remember. It suddenly came to him that he had read a few days before of Mrs. Abraham Lincoln's arrival in New York at Doctor Holbrook's sanitarium. Thither Edward went; and within half an hour from the time he had been talking with General Grant he was sitting at the bedside of Mrs. Lincoln, showing her the wonderful photograph just presented to him. Edward saw that the widow of the great Lincoln did not mentally respond to his pleasure in his possession. It was apparent even to the boy that mental and physical illness had done their work with the frail frame. But he had the memory, at least, of having got that close to the great President.

The eventful evening, however, was not yet over. Edward had boarded a Broadway stage to take him to his Brooklyn home when, glancing at the newspaper of a man sitting next to him, he saw the headline: "Jefferson Davis arrives in New York." He read enough to see that the Confederate President was stopping at the Metropolitan Hotel, in lower Broadway, and as he looked out of the stage-window the sign "Metropolitan Hotel" stared him in the face. In a moment he was out of the stage; he wrote a little note, asked the clerk to send it to Mr. Davis, and within five minutes was talking to the Confederate President and telling of his remarkable evening.

Mr. Davis was keenly interested in the coincidence and in the boy before him. He asked about the famous collec-

tion, and promised to secure for Edward a letter written by
each member of the Confederate Cabinet. This he subsequently did. Edward remained with Mr. Davis until
ten o'clock, and that evening brought about an interchange
of letters between the Brooklyn boy and Mr. Davis at Beau-
voir, Mississippi, that lasted until the latter passed away.

Edward was fast absorbing a tremendous quantity of
biographical information about the most famous men and
women of his time, and he was compiling a collection of
autograph letters that the newspapers had made famous
throughout the country. He was ruminating over his pos-
sessions one day, and wondering to what practical use he
could put his collection; for while it was proving educative
to a wonderful degree, it was, after all, a hobby, and a
hobby means expense. His autograph quest cost him sta-
tionery, postage, car-fare—all outgo. But it had brought
him no income, save a rich mental revenue. And the boy
and his family needed money. He did not know, then,
the value of a background.

He was thinking along this line in a restaurant when a
man sitting next to him opened a box of cigarettes, and taking a picture out of it threw it on the floor. Edward picked
it up, thinking it might be a "prospect" for his collection
of autograph letters. It was the picture of a well-known
actress. He then recalled an advertisement announcing
that this particular brand of cigarettes contained, in each
package, a lithographed portrait of some famous actor or
actress, and that if the purchaser would collect these he
would, in the end, have a valuable album of the greatest
actors and actresses of the day. Edward turned the picture over, only to find a blank reverse side. "All very
well," he thought, "but what does a purchaser have, after
all, in the end, but a lot of pictures? Why don't they use

the back of each picture, and tell what each did: a little biography? Then it would be worth keeping." With his passion for self-education, the idea appealed very strongly to him; and believing firmly that there were others possessed of the same thirst, he set out the next day, in his luncheon hour, to find out who made the picture.

At the office of the cigarette company he learned that the making of the pictures was in the hands of the Knapp Lithographic Company. The following luncheon hour, Edward sought the offices of the company, and explained his idea to Mr. Joseph P. Knapp, now the president of the American Lithograph Company.

"I'll give you ten dollars apiece if you will write me a one-hundred-word biography of one hundred famous Americans," was Mr. Knapp's instant reply. "Send me a list, and group them, as, for instance: presidents and vice-presidents, famous soldiers, actors, authors, etc."

"And thus," says Mr. Knapp, as he tells the tale to-day, "I gave Edward Bok his first literary commission, and started him off on his literary career."

And it is true.

But Edward soon found the Lithograph Company calling for "copy," and, write as he might, he could not supply the biographies fast enough. He, at last, completed the first hundred, and so instantaneous was their success that Mr. Knapp called for a second hundred, and then for a third. Finding that one hand was not equal to the task, Edward offered his brother five dollars for each biography; he made the same offer to one or two journalists whom he knew and whose accuracy he could trust; and he was speedily convinced that merely to edit biographies written by others, at one-half the price paid to him, was more profitable than to write himself.

So with five journalists working at top speed to supply the hungry lithograph presses, Mr. Knapp was likewise responsible for Edward Bok's first adventure as an editor. It was commercial, if you will, but it was a commercial editing that had a distinct educational value to a large public.

The important point is that Edward Bok was being led more and more to writing and to editorship.

CHAPTER IV

A PRESIDENTIAL FRIEND AND A BOSTON PILGRIMAGE

Edward Bok had not been office boy long before he realized that if he learned shorthand he would stand a better chance for advancement. So he joined the Young Men's Christian Association in Brooklyn, and entered the class in stenography. But as this class met only twice a week, Edward, impatient to learn the art of "pothooks" as quickly as possible, supplemented this instruction by a course given on two other evenings at moderate cost by a Brooklyn business college. As the system taught in both classes was the same, more rapid progress was possible, and the two teachers were constantly surprised that he acquired the art so much more quickly than the other students.

Before many weeks Edward could "stenograph" fairly well, and as the typewriter had not then come into its own, he was ready to put his knowledge to practical use.

An opportunity offered itself when the city editor of the *Brooklyn Eagle* asked him to report two speeches at a New England Society dinner. The speakers were to be President Hayes, General Grant, General Sherman, Mr. Evarts, and General Sheridan. Edward was to report what General Grant and the President said, and was instructed to give the President's speech verbatim.

At the close of the dinner, the reporters came in and Edward was seated directly in front of the President. In those days when a public dinner included several kinds of wine, it was the custom to serve the reporters with wine, and as the glasses were placed before Edward's plate he realized that he had to make a decision then and there. He had, of course, constantly seen wine on his father's table, as is the European custom, but the boy had never tasted it. He decided he would not begin then, when he needed a clear head. So, in order to get more room for his note-book, he asked the waiter to remove the glasses.

It was the first time he had ever attempted to report a public address. General Grant's remarks were few, as usual, and as he spoke slowly, he gave the young reporter no trouble. But alas for his stenographic knowledge, when President Hayes began to speak! Edward worked hard, but the President was too rapid for him; he did not get the speech, and he noticed that the reporters for the other papers fared no better. Nothing daunted, however, after the speechmaking, Edward resolutely sought the President, and as the latter turned to him, he told him his plight, ex-plained it was his first important "assignment," and asked if he could possibly be given a copy of the speech so that he could "beat" the other papers.

The President looked at him curiously for a moment, and then said: "Can you wait a few minutes?"

Edward assured him that he could.

After fifteen minutes or so the President came up to where the boy was waiting, and said abruptly:

"Tell me, my boy, why did you have the wine-glasses removed from your place?"

Edward was completely taken aback at the question, but he explained his resolution as well as he could.

"Did you make that decision this evening?" the Presi-dent asked.

He had.

"What is your name?" the President next inquired.

He was told.

"And you live, where?"

Edward told him.

"Suppose you write your name and address on this card for me," said the President, reaching for one of the place-cards on the table.

The boy did so.

"Now, I am stopping with Mr. A. A. Low, on Columbia Heights. Is that in the direction of your home?"

It was.

"Suppose you go with me, then, in my carriage," said the President, "and I will give you my speech."

Edward was not quite sure now whether he was on his head or his feet.

As he drove along with the President and his host, the President asked the boy about himself, what he was doing, etc. On arriving at Mr. Low's house, the President went up-stairs, and in a few moments came down with his speech in full, written in his own hand. Edward assured him he would copy it, and return the manuscript in the morning.

The President took out his watch. It was then after midnight. Musing a moment, he said: "You say you are an office boy; what time must you be at your office?"

"Half past eight, sir."

"Well, good night," he said, and then, as if it were a second thought: "By the way, I can get another copy of the speech. Just turn that in as it is, if they can read it."

Afterward, Edward found out that, as a matter of fact, it was the President's only copy. Though the boy did not then appreciate this act of consideration, his instinct fortunately led him to copy the speech and leave the original at the President's stopping-place in the morning.

And for all his trouble, the young reporter was amply

repaid by seeing that *The Eagle* was the only paper which had a verbatim report of the President's speech.

But the day was not yet done!

That evening, upon reaching home, what was the boy's astonishment to find the following note:

MY DEAR YOUNG FRIEND:—
I have been telling Mrs. Hayes this morning of what you told me at the dinner last evening, and she was very much interested. She would like to see you, and joins me in asking if you will call upon us this evening at eight-thirty.
                        Very faithfully yours,
                              RUTHERFORD B. HAYES.

Edward had not risen to the possession of a suit of evening clothes, and distinctly felt its lack for this occasion. But, dressed in the best he had, he set out, at eight o'clock, to call on the President of the United States and his wife!

He had no sooner handed his card to the butler than that dignitary, looking at it, announced: "The President and Mrs. Hayes are waiting for you!" The ring of those magic words still sounds in Edward's ears: "The President and Mrs. Hayes are waiting for you!"—and he a boy of sixteen!

Edward had not been in the room ten minutes before he was made to feel as thoroughly at ease as if he were sitting in his own home before an open fire with his father and mother. Skilfully the President drew from him the story of his youthful hopes and ambitions, and before the boy knew it he was telling the President and his wife all about his precious *Encyclopædia*, his evening with General Grant, and his efforts to become something more than an office boy. No boy had ever so gracious a listener before; no

mother could have been more tenderly motherly than the
woman who sat opposite him and seemed so honestly interested in all that he told.   Not for a moment during all
those two hours was he allowed to remember that his host
and hostess were the President of the United States and
the first lady of the land!

That evening was the first of many thus spent as the
years rolled by; unexpected little courtesies came from the
White House, and later from "Spiegel Grove"; a constant
and unflagging interest followed each undertaking on which
the boy embarked.   Opportunities were opened to him;
acquaintances were made possible; a letter came almost
every month until that last little note, late in 1892:

My dear Friend:
   I would write you more fully if I could.   You are always
thoughtful and kind.   Thankfully your friend,
                              Rutherford B. Hayes.
   Thanks—thanks for your steady friendship.

The simple act of turning down his wine-glasses had
won for Edward Bok two gracious friends.

The passion for autograph collecting was now leading
Edward to read the authors whom he read about.   He had
become attached to the works of the New England group:
Longfellow, Holmes, and, particularly, of Emerson.   The
philosophy of the Concord sage made a peculiarly strong
appeal to the young mind, and a small copy of Emerson's
essays was always in Edward's pocket on his long stage or
horse-car rides to his office and back.

He noticed that these New England authors rarely
visited New York, or, if they did, their presence was not
heralded by the newspapers among the "distinguished
arrivals."   He had a great desire personally to meet these

writers; and, having saved a little money, he decided to take his week's summer vacation in the winter, when he knew he should be more likely to find the people of his quest at home, and to spend his savings on a trip to Boston. He had never been so far away from home, so this trip was a momentous affair.

He arrived in Boston on Sunday evening; and the first thing he did was to despatch a note, by messenger, to Doctor Oliver Wendell Holmes, announcing the important fact that he was there, and what his errand was, and asking whether he might come up and see Doctor Holmes any time the next day. Edward naïvely told him that he could come as early as Doctor Holmes liked—by breakfast-time, he was assured, as Edward was all alone! Doctor Holmes's amusement at this ingenuous note may be imagined.

Within the hour the messenger brought back this answer:

MY DEAR BOY:
I shall certainly look for you to-morrow morning at eight o'clock to have a piece of pie with me. That is real New England, you know.
Very cordially yours,
OLIVER WENDELL HOLMES.

Edward was there at eight o'clock. Strictly speaking, he was there at seven-thirty, and found the author already at his desk in that room overlooking the Charles River.

"Well," was the cheery greeting, "you couldn't wait until eight for your breakfast, could you? Neither could I when I was a boy. I used to have my breakfast at seven," and then telling the boy all about his boyhood, the cheery poet led him to the dining-room, and for the first time he breakfasted away from home and ate pie—and that with "The Autocrat" at his own breakfast-table!

A cosier time no boy could have had. Just the two were there, and the smiling face that looked out over the plates and cups gave the boy courage to tell all that this trip was going to mean to him.

"And you have come on just to see us, have you?" chuckled the poet. "Now, tell me, what good do you think you will get out of it?"

He was told what the idea was: that every successful man had something to tell a boy, that would be likely to help him, and that Edward wanted to see the men who had written the books that people enjoyed. Doctor Holmes could not conceal his amusement at all this.

When breakfast was finished, Doctor Holmes said: "Do you know that I am a full-fledged carpenter? No? Well, I am. Come into my carpenter-shop."

And he led the way into a front-basement room where was a complete carpenter's outfit.

"You know I am a doctor," he explained, "and this shop is my medicine. I believe that every man must have a hobby that is as different from his regular work as it is possible to be. It is not good for a man to work all the time at one thing. So this is my hobby. This is my change. I like to putter away at these things. Every day I try to come down here for an hour or so. It rests me because it gives my mind a complete change. For, whether you believe it or not," he added with his inimitable chuckle, "to make a poem and to make a chair are two very different things.

"Now," he continued, "if you think you can learn something from me, learn that and remember it when you are a man. Don't keep always at your business, whatever it may be. It makes no difference how much you like it. The more you like it, the more dangerous it is. When you grow up you will understand what I mean by an 'outlet'—a hobby, that is—in your life, and it must be so different from your regular work that it will take your thoughts into an entirely different direction. We doctors call it a safety-valve, and it is. I would much rather," concluded the poet, "you would forget all that I have ever written than that you should forget what I tell you about having a safety-valve."

"And now do you know," smilingly said the poet, "about the Charles River here?" as they returned to his study and stood before the large bay window. "I love this river," he said. "Yes, I love it," he repeated; "love it in summer or in winter." And then he was quiet for a minute or so.

Edward asked him which of his poems were his favorites.

"Well," he said musingly, "I think 'The Chambered Nautilus' is my most finished piece of work, and I suppose it is my favorite. But there are also 'The Voiceless,' 'My Aviary,' written at this window, 'The Battle of Bunker Hill,' and 'Dorothy Q,' written to the portrait of my great-grandmother which you see on the wall there. All these I have a liking for, and when I speak of the poems I like best there are two others that ought to be included—'The Silent Melody' and 'The Last Leaf.' I think these are among my best."

"What is the history of 'The Chambered Nautilus'?" Edward asked.

"It has none," came the reply, "it wrote itself. So, too, did 'The One-Hoss Shay.' That was one of those random conceptions that gallop through the brain, and that you catch by the bridle. I caught it and reined it. That is all."

Just then a maid brought in a parcel, and as Doctor

Holmes opened it on his desk he smiled over at the boy and said:

"Well, I declare, if you haven't come just at the right time. See those little books? Aren't they wee?" and he handed the boy a set of three little books, six inches by four in size, beautifully bound in half levant. They were his "Autocrat" in one volume, and his better-known poems in two volumes.

"This is a little fancy of mine," he said. "My publishers, to please me, have gotten out this tiny wee set. And here," as he counted the little sets, "they have sent me six sets. Are they not exquisite little things?" and he fondled them with loving glee. "Lucky, too, for me that they should happen to come now, for I have been wondering what I could give you as a souvenir of your visit to me, and here it is, sure enough! My publishers must have guessed you were here and my mind at the same time. Now, if you would like it, you shall carry home one of these little sets, and I'll just write a piece from one of my poems and your name on the fly-leaf of each volume. You say you like that little verse:

"'A few can touch the magic string.'

Then I'll write those four lines in this volume." And he did.

> A few can touch the magic string,
>   And noisy Fame is proud to win them,—
> Alas for those who never sing,
>   But die with all their music in them!
>   OLIVER WENDELL HOLMES.

As each little volume went under the poet's pen Edward said, as his heart swelled in gratitude:

"Doctor Holmes, you are a man of the rarest sort to be so good to a boy."

The pen stopped, the poet looked out on the Charles a moment, and then, turning to the boy with a little moisture in his eye, he said:

"No, my boy, I am not; but it does an old man's heart good to hear you say it. It means much to those on the down-hill side to be well thought of by the young who are coming up."

As he wiped his gold pen, with its swan-quill holder, and laid it down, he said:

"That's the pen with which I wrote 'Elsie Venner' and the 'Autocrat' papers. I try to take care of it."

"You say you are going from me over to see Longfellow?" he continued, as he reached out once more for the pen. "Well, then, would you mind if I gave you a letter for him? I have something to send him."

Sly but kindly old gentleman! The "something" he had to send Longfellow was Edward himself, although the boy did not see through the subterfuge at that time.

"And now, if you are going, I'll walk along with you if you don't mind, for I'm going down to Park Street to thank my publishers for these little books, and that lies along your way to the Cambridge car."

As the two walked along Beacon Street, Doctor Holmes pointed out the residences where lived people of interest, and when they reached the Public Garden he said:

"You must come over in the spring some time, and see the tulips and croci and hyacinths here. They are so beautiful.

"Now, here is your car," he said as he hailed a coming horse-car. "Before you go back you must come and see me and tell me all the people you have seen, will you? I should like to hear about them. I may not have more books coming in, but I might have a very good-looking photograph of a very old-looking little man," he said as his eyes twinkled. "Give my love to Longfellow when you see him, and don't forget to give him my letter, you know. It is about a very important matter."

And when the boy had ridden a mile or so with his fare in his hand he held it out to the conductor, who grinned and said:

"That's all right. Doctor Holmes paid me your fare, and I'm going to keep that nickel if I lose my job for it."

CHAPTER V

GOING TO THE THEATRE WITH LONGFELLOW

When Edward Bok stood before the home of Longfellow, he realized that he was to see the man around whose head the boy's youthful reading had cast a sort of halo. And when he saw the head itself he had a feeling that he could see the halo. No kindlier pair of eyes ever looked at a boy, as, with a smile, "the white Mr. Longfellow," as Mr. Howells had called him, held out his hand.

"I am very glad to see you, my boy," were his first words, and with them he won the boy. Edward smiled back at the poet, and immediately the two were friends.

"I have been taking a walk this beautiful morning," he said next, "and am a little late getting at my mail. Suppose you come in and sit at my desk with me, and we will see what the postman has brought. He brings me so many good things, you know."

"Now, here is a little girl," he said, as he sat down at the desk with the boy beside him, "who wants my autograph and a 'sentiment.' What sentiment, I wonder, shall I send her?"

"Why not send her 'Let us, then, be up and doing'?" suggested the boy. "That's what I should like if I were she."

"Should you, indeed?" said Longfellow. "That is a good suggestion. Now, suppose you recite it off to me, so that I shall not have to look it up in my books, and I will

37

write as you recite. But slowly; you know I am an old man, and write slowly."

Edward thought it strange that Longfellow himself should not know his own great words without looking them up. But he recited the four lines, so familiar to every schoolboy, and when the poet had finished writing them, he said:

"Good! I see you have a memory. Now, suppose I copy these lines once more for the little girl, and give you this copy? Then you can say, you know, that you dictated my own poetry to me."

Of course Edward was delighted, and Longfellow gave him the sheet on which he had written:

> Let us, then, be up and doing,
>   With a heart, for any fate;
> Still achieving, still pursuing,
>   Learn to labor and to wait.
>   HENRY W. LONGFELLOW.

Then, as the fine head bent down to copy the lines once more, Edward ventured to say to him:

"I should think it would keep you busy if you did this for every one who asked you."

"Well," said the poet, "you see, I am not so busy a man as I was some years ago, and I shouldn't like to disappoint a little girl, should you?"

As he took up his letters again, he discovered five more requests for his autograph. At each one he reached into a drawer in his desk, took a card, and wrote his name on it.

"There are a good many of these every day," said Longfellow, "but I always like to do this little favor. It is so little to do, to write your name on a card; and if I didn't do it some boy or girl might be looking, day by day, for the postman and be disappointed. I only wish I could write my name better for them. You see how I break my letters? That's because I never took pains with my writing when I was a boy. I don't think I should get a high mark for penmanship if I were at school, do you?"

"I see you get letters from Europe," said the boy, as Longfellow opened an envelope with a foreign stamp on it.

"Yes, from all over the world," said the poet. Then, looking at the boy quickly, he said: "Do you collect postage-stamps?"

Edward said he did.

"Well, I have some right here, then," and going to a drawer in a desk he took out a bundle of letters, and cut out the postage-stamps and gave them to the boy.

"There's one from the Netherlands. There's where I was born," Edward ventured to say.

"In the Netherlands? Then you are a real Dutchman. Well! Well!" he said, laying down his pen. "Can you read Dutch?"

The boy said he could.

"Then," said the poet, "you are just the boy I am looking for." And going to a bookcase behind him he brought out a book, and handing it to the boy, he said, his eyes laughing: "Can you read that?"

"Yes, indeed," said Edward. "These are your poems in Dutch."

"That's right," he said. "Now, this is delightful. I am so glad you came. I received this book last week, and although I have been in the Netherlands, I cannot speak or read Dutch. I wonder whether you would read a poem to me and let me hear how it sounds."

So Edward took "The Old Clock on the Stairs," and read it to him.

The poet's face beamed with delight. "That's beauti-ful," he said, and then quickly added: "I mean the lan-guage, not the poem."

"Now," he went on, "I'll tell you what we'll do: we'll strike a bargain. We Yankees are great for bargains, you know. If you will read me 'The Village Blacksmith' you can sit in that chair there made out of the wood of the old spreading chestnut-tree, and I'll take you out and show you where the old shop stood. Is that a bargain?"

Edward assured him it was. He sat in the chair of wood and leather, and read to the poet several of his own poems in a language in which, when he wrote them, he never dreamed they would ever be printed. He was very quiet. Finally he said: "It seems so odd, so very odd, to hear something you know so well sound so strange."

"It's a great compliment, though, isn't it, sir?" asked the boy.

"Ye-es," said the poet slowly. "Yes, yes," he added quickly. "It is, my boy, a very great compliment."

"Ah," he said, rousing himself, as a maid appeared, "that means luncheon, or rather, it means dinner, for we have dinner in the old New England fashion, in the middle of the day. I am all alone to-day, and you must keep me company, will you? Then afterward we'll go and take a walk, and I'll show you Cambridge. It is such a beautiful old town, even more beautiful, I sometimes think, when the leaves are off the trees.

"Come," he said, "I'll take you up-stairs, and you can wash your hands in the room where George Washington slept. And comb your hair, too, if you want to," he added; "only it isn't the same comb that he used."

To the boyish mind it was an historic breaking of bread, that midday meal with Longfellow.

EDWARD BOK'S BIRTHPLACE AT HELDER, NETHERLANDS

In the foreground is one of the typical Dutch canals; at the end of the garden in the rear is one of the famous Dutch dykes and just beyond is the North Sea. The house now belongs to the Dutch Government

"Can you say grace in Dutch?" he asked, as they sat down; and the boy did.

"Well," the poet declared, "I never expected to hear that at my table. I like the sound of it."

Then while the boy told all that he knew about the Netherlands, the poet told the boy all about his poems. Edward said he liked "Hiawatha."

"So do I," he said. "But I think I like 'Evangeline' better. Still, neither one is as good as it should be. But those are the things you see afterward so much better than you do at the time."

It was a great event for Edward when, with the poet nodding and smiling to every boy and man he met, and lifting his hat to every woman and little girl, he walked through the fine old streets of Cambridge with Longfellow. At one point of the walk they came to a theatrical billboard announcing an attraction that evening at the Boston Theatre. Skilfully the old poet drew out from Edward that sometimes he went to the theatre with his parents. As they returned to the gate of "Craigie House" Edward said he thought he would go back to Boston.

"And what have you on hand for this evening?" asked Longfellow.

Edward told him he was going to his hotel to think over the day's events.

The poet laughed and said:

"Now, listen to my plan. Boston is strange to you. Now we're going to the theatre this evening, and my plan is that you come in now, have a little supper with us, and then go with us to see the play. It is a funny play, and a good laugh will do you more good than to sit in a hotel all by yourself. Now, what do you think?"

Of course the boy thought as Longfellow did, and it was

a very happy boy that evening who, in full view of the large audience in the immense theatre, sat in that box. It was, as Longfellow had said, a play of laughter, and just who laughed louder, the poet or the boy, neither ever knew.

Between the acts there came into the box a man of courtly presence, dignified and yet gently courteous.

"Ah! Phillips," said the poet, "how are you? You must know my young friend here. This is Wendell Phillips, my boy. Here is a young man who told me to-day that he was going to call on you and on Phillips Brooks to-morrow. Now you know him before he comes to you."

"I shall be glad to see you, my boy," said Mr. Phillips. "And so you are going to see Phillips Brooks? Let me tell you something about Brooks. He has a great many books in his library which are full of his marks and comments. Now, when you go to see him you ask him to let you see some of those books, and then, when he isn't looking, you put a couple of them in your pocket. They would make splendid souvenirs, and he has so many he would never miss them. You do it, and then when you come to see me tell me all about it."

And he and Longfellow smiled broadly.

An hour later, when Longfellow dropped Edward at his hotel, he had not only a wonderful day to think over but another wonderful day to look forward to as well!

He had breakfasted with Oliver Wendell Holmes; dined, supped, and been to the theatre with Longfellow; and to-morrow he was to spend with Phillips Brooks.

Boston was a great place, Edward Bok thought, as he fell asleep.

CHAPTER VI

No one who called at Phillips Brooks's house was ever told that the master of the house was out when he was in. That was a rule laid down by Doctor Brooks: a maid was not to perjure herself for her master's comfort or convenience. Therefore, when Edward was told that Doctor Brooks was out, he knew he *was* out. The boy waited, and as he waited he had a chance to look around the library and into the books. The rector's faithful housekeeper said he might when he repeated what Wendell Phillips had told him of the interest that was to be found in her master's books. Edward did not tell her of Mr. Phillips's advice to "borrow" a couple of books. He reserved that bit of information for the rector of Trinity when he came in, an hour later.

"Oh! did he?" laughingly said Doctor Brooks. "That is nice advice for a man to give a boy. I am surprised at Wendell Phillips. He needs a little talk: a ministerial visit. And have you followed his shameless advice?" smilingly asked the huge man as he towered above the boy. "No? And to think of the opportunity you had, too. Well, I am glad you had such respect for my dumb friends. For they are my friends, each one of them," he continued, as he looked fondly at the filled shelves. "Yes, I know them all, and love each for its own sake. Take this little volume," and he picked up a little volume of Shakespeare. "Why, we are the best of friends: we have travelled miles together—all over the world, as a matter of fact. It knows me in all my moods, and responds to each, no matter how irritable I am. Yes, it is pretty badly marked up now, for a fact, isn't it? Black; I never thought of that before that it doesn't make a book look any better to the eye. But it means more to me because of all that pencilling.

"Now, some folks dislike my use of my books in this way. They love their books so much that they think it nothing short of sacrilege to mark up a book. But to me that's like having a child so prettily dressed that you can't romp and play with it. What is the good of a book, I say, if it is too pretty for use? I like to have my books speak to me, and then I like to talk back to them.

"Take my Bible, here," he continued, as he took up an old and much-worn copy of the book. "I have a number of copies of the Great Book: one copy I preach from; another I minister from; but this is my own personal copy, and into it I talk and talk. See how I talk," and he opened the Book and showed interleaved pages full of comments in his handwriting. "There's where St. Paul and I had an argument one day. Yes, it was a long argument, and I don't know now who won," he added smilingly. "But then, no one ever wins in an argument, anyway, do you think so?

"You see," went on the preacher, "I put into these books what other men put into articles and essays for magazines and papers. I never write for publications. I always think of my church when something comes to me to say. There is always danger of a man spreading himself out thin if he attempts too much, you know."

Doctor Brooks must have caught the boy's eye, which, as he said this, naturally surveyed his great frame, for he regarded him in an amused way, and putting his hands on his girth, he said laughingly: "You are thinking I would have to do a great deal to spread myself out thin, aren't you?"

The boy confessed he was, and the preacher laughed one of those deep laughs of his that were so infectious.

"But here I am talking about myself. Tell me something about *yourself?*"

And when the boy told his object in coming to Boston, the rector of Trinity Church was immensely amused.

"Just to see us fellows! Well, and how do you like us so far?"

And in the most comfortable way this true gentleman went on until the boy mentioned that he must be keeping him from his work.

"Not at all; not at all," was the quick and hearty response. "Not a thing to do. I cleaned up all my mail before I had my breakfast this morning.

"These letters, you mean?" he said, as the boy pointed to some letters on his desk unopened. "Oh, yes! They must have come in a later mail. Well, if it will make you feel any better I'll go through them, and you can go through my books if you like. I'll trust you," he added laughingly, as Wendell Phillips's advice occurred to him.

"You like books, you say?" he went on, as he opened his letters. "Well, then, you must come into my library here at any time you are in Boston, and spend a morning reading anything I have that you like. Young men do that, you know, and I like to have them. What's the use of good friends if you don't share them? There's where the pleasure comes in."

He asked the boy then about his newspaper work, how much it paid him, and whether he felt it helped him in an educational way. The boy told him he thought it did; that it furnished good lessons in the study of human nature.

"Yes," he said, "I can believe that, so long as it is good journalism."

As he let the boy out of his house, at the end of that first meeting, he said to him:

"And you're going from me now to see Emerson? I don't know," he added reflectively, "whether you will see him at his best. Still, you may. And even if you do not, to have seen him, even as you may see him, is better, in a way, than not to have seen him at all."

Edward did not know what Phillips Brooks meant. But he was, sadly, to find out the next day.

A boy was pretty sure of a welcome from Louisa Alcott, and his greeting from her was spontaneous and sincere.

"Why, you good boy," she said, "to come all the way to Concord to see us," quite for all the world as if she were the one favored. "Now take your coat off, and come right in by the fire. Do tell me all about your visit."

Before that cozy fire they chatted. It was pleasant to the boy to sit there with that sweet-faced woman with those kindly eyes! After a while she said: "Now I shall put on my coat and hat, and we shall walk over to Emerson's house. I am almost afraid to promise that you will see him. He sees scarcely any one now. He is feeble, and—" She did not finish the sentence. "But we'll walk over there, at any rate."

She spoke mostly of her father as the two walked along, and it was easy to see that his condition was now the one thought of her life. Presently they reached Emerson's house, and Miss Emerson welcomed them at the door. After a brief chat Miss Alcott told of the boy's hope. Miss Emerson shook her head.

"Father sees no one now," she said, "and I fear it might not be a pleasure if you did see him."

Then Edward told her what Phillips Brooks had said.

"Well," she said, "I'll see."

She had scarcely left the room when Miss Alcott rose and followed her, saying to the boy: "You shall see Mr. Emerson if it is at all possible."

In a few minutes Miss Alcott returned, her eyes moistened, and simply said: "Come."

The boy followed her through two rooms, and at the threshold of the third, Miss Emerson stood, also with moistened eyes.

"Father," she said simply, and there, at his desk, sat Emerson—the man whose words had already won Edward Bok's boyish interest, and who was destined to impress himself upon his life more deeply than any other writer.

Slowly, at the daughter's spoken word, Emerson rose with a wonderful quiet dignity, extended his hand, and as the boy's hand rested in his, looked him full in the eyes.

No light of welcome came from those sad yet tender eyes. The boy closed upon the hand in his with a loving pressure, and for a single moment the eyelids rose, a different look came into those eyes, and Edward felt a slight, perceptible response of the hand. But that was all!

Quietly he motioned the boy to a chair beside the desk. Edward sat down and was about to say something, when, instead of seating himself, Emerson walked away to the window and stood there softly whistling and looking out as if there were no one in the room. Edward's eyes had followed Emerson's every footstep, when the boy was aroused by hearing a suppressed sob, and as he looked around he saw that it came from Miss Emerson. Slowly she walked out of the room. The boy looked at Miss

Alcott, and she put her finger to her mouth, indicating silence. He was nonplussed.

Edward looked toward Emerson standing in that window, and wondered what it all meant. Presently Emerson left the window and, crossing the room, came to his desk, bowing to the boy as he passed, and seated himself, not speaking a word and ignoring the presence of the two persons in the room.

Suddenly the boy heard Miss Alcott say: "Have you read this new book by Ruskin yet?"

Slowly the great master of thought lifted his eyes from his desk, turned toward the speaker, rose with stately courtesy from his chair, and, bowing to Miss Alcott, said with great deliberation: "Did you speak to me, madam?"

The boy was dumfounded! Louisa Alcott, his Louisa! And he did not know her! Suddenly the whole sad truth flashed upon the boy. Tears sprang into Miss Alcott's eyes, and she walked to the other side of the room. The boy did not know what to say or do, so he sat silent. With a deliberate movement Emerson resumed his seat, and slowly his eyes roamed over the boy sitting at the side of the desk. He felt he should say something.

"I thought, perhaps, Mr. Emerson," he said, "that you might be able to favor me with a letter from Carlyle."

At the mention of the name Carlyle his eyes lifted, and he asked: "Carlyle, did you say, sir, Carlyle?"

"Yes," said the boy, "Thomas Carlyle."

"Ye-es," Emerson answered slowly. "To be sure, Carlyle. Yes, he was here this morning. He will be here again to-morrow morning," he added gleefully, almost like a child.

Then suddenly: "You were saying——"

Edward repeated his request.

"Oh, I think so, I think so," said Emerson, to the boy's astonishment. "Let me see. Yes, here in this drawer I have many letters from Carlyle."

At these words Miss Alcott came from the other part of the room, her wet eyes dancing with pleasure and her face wreathed in smiles.

"I think we can help this young man; do you not think so, Louisa?" said Emerson, smiling toward Miss Alcott. The whole atmosphere of the room had changed. How different the expression of his eyes as now Emerson looked at the boy! "And you have come all the way from New York to ask me that!" he said smilingly as the boy told him of his trip. "Now, let us see," he said, as he delved in a drawer full of letters.

For a moment he groped among letters and papers, and then, softly closing the drawer, he began that ominous low whistle once more, looked inquiringly at each, and dropped his eyes straightway to the papers before him on his desk. It was to be only for a few moments, then! Miss Alcott turned away.

The boy felt the interview could not last much longer. So, anxious to have some personal souvenir of the meeting, he said: "Mr. Emerson, will you be so good as to write your name in this book for me?" and he brought out an album he had in his pocket.

"Name?" he asked vaguely.

"Yes, please," said the boy, "your name: Ralph Waldo Emerson."

But the sound of the name brought no response from the eyes.

"Please write out the name you want," he said finally, "and I will copy it for you if I can."

It was hard for the boy to believe his own senses. But

picking up a pen he wrote: "Ralph Waldo Emerson, Concord; November 22, 1881."

Emerson looked at it, and said mournfully: "Thank you." Then he picked up the pen, and writing the single letter "R" stopped, followed his finger until it reached the 'W" of Waldo, and studiously copied letter by letter! At the word "Concord" he seemed to hesitate, as if the task were too great, but finally copied again, letter by letter, until the second "c" was reached. "Another 'o,'" he said, and interpolated an extra letter in the name of the town which he had done so much to make famous the world over. When he had finished he handed back the book, in which there was written:

R. Waldo Emerson
Concord
November 22, 1881

The boy put the book into his pocket; and as he did so Emerson's eye caught the slip on his desk, in the boy's handwriting, and, with a smile of absolute enlightenment, he turned and said:

"You wish me to write my name? With pleasure. Have you a book with you?"

Overcome with astonishment, Edward mechanically handed him the album once more from his pocket. Quickly turning over the leaves, Emerson picked up the pen, and pushing aside the slip, wrote without a moment's hesitation:

Ralph Waldo Emerson
Concord

The boy was almost dazed at the instantaneous transformation in the man!

Miss Alcott now grasped this moment to say: "Well, we must be going!"

"So soon?" said Emerson, rising and smiling. Then turning to Miss Alcott he said: "It was very kind of you, Louisa, to run over this morning and bring your young friend."

Then turning to the boy he said: "Thank you so much for coming to see me. You must come over again while you are with the Alcotts. Good morning! Isn't it a beautiful day out?" he said, and as he shook the boy's hand there was a warm grasp in it, the fingers closed around those of the boy, and as Edward looked into those deep eyes they twinkled and smiled back.

The going was all so different from the coming. The boy was grateful that his last impression was of a moment when the eye kindled and the hand pulsated.

The two walked back to the Alcott home in an almost unbroken silence. Once Edward ventured to remark:

"You can have no idea, Miss Alcott, how grateful I am to you."

"Well, my boy," she answered, "Phillips Brooks may be right: that it is something to have seen him even so, than not to have seen him at all. But to us it is so *sad*, so very sad. The twilight is gently closing in."

And so it proved—just five months afterward.

Eventful day after eventful day followed in Edward's Boston visit. The following morning he spent with Wendell Phillips, who presented him with letters from William Lloyd Garrison, Lucretia Mott, and other famous persons; and then, writing a letter of introduction to Charles Francis Adams, whom he enjoined to give the boy autograph letters from his two presidential forbears, John Adams and John Quincy Adams, sent Edward on his way rejoicing. Mr. Adams received the boy with equal graciousness and liberality. Wonderful letters from the two Adamses were his when he left.

And then, taking the train for New York, Edward Bok went home, sitting up all night in a day-coach for the double purpose of saving the cost of a sleeping-berth and of having a chance to classify and clarify the events of the most wonderful week in his life!

CHAPTER VII

The father of Edward Bok passed away when Edward was eighteen years of age, and it was found that the amount of the small insurance left behind would barely cover the funeral expenses. Hence the two boys faced the problem of supporting the mother on their meagre income. They determined to have but one goal: to put their mother back to that life of comfort to which she had been brought up and was formerly accustomed. But that was not possible on their income. It was evident that other employment must be taken on during the evenings.

The city editor of the *Brooklyn Eagle* had given Edward the assignment of covering the news of the theatres; he was to ascertain "coming attractions" and any other dramatic items of news interest. One Monday evening, when a multiplicity of events crowded the reportorial corps, Edward was delegated to "cover" the Grand Opera House, where Rose Coghlan was to appear in a play that had already been seen in Brooklyn, and called, therefore, for no special dramatic criticism. Yet *The Eagle* wanted to cover it. It so happened that Edward had made another appointment for that evening which he considered more important, and yet not wishing to disappoint his editor he accepted the assignment. He had seen Miss Coghlan in the play; so he kept his other engagement, and without approaching the theatre he wrote a notice to the effect that Miss Coghlan acted her part, if anything, with greater power than on her previous Brooklyn visit, and so forth, and handed it in to his city editor the next morning on his way to business.

Unfortunately, however, Miss Coghlan had been taken ill just before the raising of the curtain, and, there being no understudy, no performance had been given and the audience dismissed. All this was duly commented upon by the New York morning newspapers. Edward read this bit of news on the ferry-boat, but his notice was in the hands of the city editor.

On reaching home that evening he found a summons from *The Eagle*, and the next morning he received a rebuke, and was informed that his chances with the paper were over. The ready acknowledgment and evident regret of the crestfallen boy, however, appealed to the editor, and before the end of the week he called the boy to him and promised him another chance, provided the lesson had sunk in. It had, and it left a lasting impression. It was always a cause of profound gratitude with Edward Bok that his first attempt at "faking" occurred so early in his journalistic career that he could take the experience to heart and profit by it.

One evening when Edward was attending a theatrical performance, he noticed the restlessness of the women in the audience between the acts. In those days it was, even more than at present, the custom for the men to go out between the acts, leaving the women alone. Edward looked at the programme in his hands. It was a large eleven-by-nine sheet, four pages, badly printed, with nothing in it save the cast, a few advertisements, and an announcement of some coming attraction. The boy mechanically folded the programme, turned it long side up and wondered whether a programme of this smaller size, easier to handle, with an attractive cover and some reading-matter, would not be profitable.

When he reached home he made up an eight-page

"dummy," pasted an attractive picture on the cover, indicated the material to go inside, and the next morning showed it to the manager of the theatre. The programme as issued was an item of considerable expense to the management; Edward offered to supply his new programme without cost, provided he was given the exclusive right, and the manager at once accepted the offer. Edward then sought a friend, Frederic L. Colver, who had a larger experience in publishing and advertising, with whom he formed a partnership. Deciding that immediately upon the issuance of their first programme the idea was likely to be taken up by the other theatres, Edward proceeded to secure the exclusive rights to them all. The two young publishers solicited their advertisements on the way to and from business mornings and evenings, and shortly the first smaller-sized theatre programme, now in use in all theatres, appeared. The venture was successful from the start, returning a comfortable profit each week. Such advertisements as they could not secure for cash they accepted in trade; and this latter arrangement assisted materially in maintaining the households of the two publishers.

Edward's partner now introduced him into a debating society called The Philomathean Society, made up of young men connected with Plymouth Church, of which Henry Ward Beecher was pastor. The debates took the form of a miniature congress, each member representing a State, and it is a curious coincidence that Edward drew, by lot, the representation of the Commonwealth of Pennsylvania. The members took these debates very seriously; no subject was too large for them to discuss. Edward became intensely interested in the society's doings, and it was not long before he was elected president.

The society derived its revenue from the dues of its

members and from an annual concert given under its aus-
pices in Plymouth Church. When the time for the concert under Edward's presidency came around, he decided
that the occasion should be unique so as to insure a
crowded house. He induced Mr. Beecher to preside; he
got General Grant's promise to come and speak; he secured
the gratuitous services of Emma C. Thursby, Annie Louise
Cary, Clara Louise Kellogg, and Evelyn Lyon Hegeman,
all of the first rank of concert-singers of that day, with the
result that the church could not accommodate the crowd
which naturally was attracted by such a programme.

It now entered into the minds of the two young theatre-
programme publishers to extend their publishing interests
by issuing an "organ" for their society, and the first issue
of *The Philomathean Review* duly appeared with Mr. Colver
as its publisher and Edward Bok as editor. Edward had
now an opportunity to try his wings in an editorial capacity. The periodical was, of course, essentially an organ of
the society; but gradually it took on a more general character, so that its circulation might extend over a larger portion of Brooklyn. With this extension came a further
broadening of its contents, which now began to take on a
literary character, and it was not long before its two pro-
jectors realized that the periodical had outgrown its name.
It was decided—late in 1884—to change the name to *The
Brooklyn Magazine*.

There was a periodical called *The Plymouth Pulpit*,
which presented verbatim reports of the sermons of Mr.
Beecher, and Edward got the idea of absorbing the *Pulpit*
in the *Magazine*. But that required more capital than he
and his partner could command. They consulted Mr.
Beecher, who, attracted by the enterprise of the two boys,
sent them with letters of introduction to a few of his most

influential parishioners, with the result that the pair soon had a sufficient financial backing by some of the leading men of Brooklyn, like H. B. Claflin, Seth Low, Rossiter W. Raymond, Horatio C. King, and others.

The young publishers could now go on. Understanding that Mr. Beecher's sermons might give a partial and denominational tone to the magazine, Edward arranged to publish also in its pages verbatim reports of the sermons of the Reverend T. De Witt Talmage, whose reputation was then at its zenith. The young editor now realized that he had a rather heavy cargo of sermons to carry each month; accordingly, in order that his magazine might not appear to be exclusively religious, he determined that its literary contents should be of a high order and equal in interest to the sermons. But this called for additional capital, and the capital furnished was not for that purpose.

It is here that Edward's autographic acquaintances stood him in good stead. He went in turn to each noted person he had met, explained his plight and stated his ambitions, with the result that very soon the magazine and the public were surprised at the distinction of the contributors to *The Brooklyn Magazine*. Each number contained a noteworthy list of them, and when an article by the President of the United States, then Rutherford B. Hayes, opened one of the numbers, the public was astonished, since up to that time the unwritten rule that a President's writings were confined to official pronouncements had scarcely been broken. William Dean Howells, General Grant, General Sherman, Phillips Brooks, General Sheridan, Canon Farrar, Cardinal Gibbons, Marion Harland, Margaret Sangster—the most prominent men and women of the day, some of whom had never written for magazines—began to appear in the young editor's contents. Editors wondered how the publishers could afford it, whereas, in fact, not a single name represented an honorarium. Each contributor had come gratuitously to the aid of the editor.

At first, the circulation of the magazine permitted the boys to wrap the copies themselves; and then they, with two other boys, would carry as huge bundles as they could lift, put them late at night on the front platform of the street-cars, and take them to the post-office. Thus the boys absolutely knew the growth of their circulation by the weight of their bundles and the number of their front-platform trips each month. Soon a baker's hand-cart was leased for an evening, and that was added to the capacity of the front platforms. Then one eventful month it was seen that a horse-truck would have to be employed. Within three weeks, a double horse-truck was necessary, and three trips had to be made.

By this time Edward Bok had become so intensely interested in the editorial problem, and his partner in the periodical publishing part, that they decided to sell out their theatre-programme interests and devote themselves to the magazine and its rapidly increasing circulation. All of Edward's editorial work had naturally to be done outside of his business hours, in other words, in the evenings and on Sundays; and the young editor found himself fully occupied. He now revived the old idea of selecting a subject and having ten or twenty writers express their views on it. It was the old symposium idea, but it had not been presented in American journalism for a number of years. He conceived the topic "Should America Have a Westminster Abbey?" and induced some twenty of the foremost men and women of the day to discuss it. When the discussion was presented in the magazine, the form being new and the theme novel, Edward was careful to send ad-

vance sheets to the newspapers, which treated it at length
in reviews and editorials, with marked effect upon the circulation of the magazine.

All this time, while Edward Bok was an editor in his
evenings he was, during the day, a stenographer and clerk
of the Western Union Telegraph Company. The two occupations were hardly compatible, but each meant a source
of revenue to the boy, and he felt he must hold on to both.

After his father passed away, the position of the boy's
desk—next to the empty desk of his father—was a cause
of constant depression to him. This was understood by
the attorney for the company, Mr. Clarence Cary, who
sought the head of Edward's department, with the result
that Edward was transferred to Mr. Cary's department
as the attorney's private stenographer.

Edward had been much attracted to Mr. Cary, and
the attorney believed in the boy, and decided to show his
interest by pushing him along. He had heard of the dual
rôle which Edward was playing; he bought a copy of the
magazine, and was interested. Edward now worked with
new zest for his employer and friend; while in every free
moment he read law, feeling that, as almost all his forbears had been lawyers, he might perhaps be destined for
the bar. This acquaintance with the fundamental basis of
law, cursory as it was, became like a gospel to Edward Bok.
In later years, he was taught its value by repeated experience in his contact with corporate laws, contracts, property
leases, and other matters; and he determined that, whatever the direction of activity taken by his sons, each should
spend at least a year in the study of law.

The control of the Western Union Telegraph Company
had now passed into the hands of Jay Gould and his com-
panions, and in the many legal matters arising therefrom,

Edward saw much, in his office, of "the little wizard of Wall Street." One day, the financier had to dictate a contract, and, coming into Mr. Cary's office, decided to dictate it then and there. An hour afterward Edward delivered the copy of the contract to Mr. Gould, and the financier was so struck by its accuracy and by the legibility of the handwriting that afterward he almost daily "happened in" to dictate to Mr. Cary's stenographer. Mr. Gould's private stenographer was in his own office in lower Broadway; but on his way down-town in the morning Mr. Gould invariably stopped at the Western Union Building, at 195 Broadway, and the habit resulted in the installation of a private office there. He borrowed Edward to do his stenography. The boy found himself taking not only letters from Mr. Gould's dictation, but, what interested him particularly, the financier's orders to buy and sell stock.

Edward watched the effects on the stock-market of these little notes which he wrote out and then shot through a pneumatic tube to Mr. Gould's brokers. Naturally, the results enthralled the boy, and he told Mr. Cary about his discoveries. This, in turn, interested Mr. Cary; Mr. Gould's dictations were frequently given in Mr. Cary's own office, where, as his desk was not ten feet from that of his stenographer, the attorney heard them, and began to buy and sell according to the magnate's decisions.

Edward had now become tremendously interested in the stock game which he saw constantly played by the great financier; and having a little money saved up, he concluded that he would follow in the wake of Mr. Gould's orders. One day, he naïvely mentioned his desire to Mr. Gould, when the financier seemed in a particularly favorable frame of mind; but Edward did not succeed in drawing out the advice he hoped for. "At least," reasoned Edward, "he knew of my intention; and if he considered it a violation of confidence he would have said as much."

Construing the financier's silence to mean at least not a prohibition, Edward went to his Sunday-school teacher, who was a member of a Wall Street brokerage firm, laid the facts before him, and asked him if he would buy for him some Western Union stock. Edward explained, however, that somehow he did not like the gambling idea of buying "on margin," and preferred to purchase the stock outright. He was shown that this would mean smaller profits; but the boy had in mind the loss of his father's fortune, brought about largely by "stock margins," and he did not intend to follow that example. So, prudently, under the brokerage of his Sunday-school teacher, and guided by the tips of no less a man than the controlling factor of stock-market finance, Edward Bok took his first plunge in Wall Street!

Of course the boy's buying and selling tallied precisely with the rise and fall of Western Union stock. It could scarcely have been otherwise. Jay Gould had the cards all in his hands; and as he bought and sold, so Edward bought and sold. The trouble was, the combination did not end there, as Edward might have foreseen had he been older and thus wiser. For as Edward bought and sold, so did his Sunday-school teacher, and all his customers who had seen the wonderful acumen of their broker in choosing exactly the right time to buy and sell Western Union. But Edward did not know this.

One day a rumor became current on the Street that an agreement had been reached by the Western Union Company and its bitter rival, the American Union Telegraph Company, whereby the former was to absorb the latter. Naturally, the report affected Western Union stock. But

Mr. Gould denied it in toto; said the report was not true, no such consolidation was in view or had even been considered. Down tumbled the stock, of course.

But it so happened that Edward knew the rumor *was* true, because Mr. Gould, some time before, had personally given him the contract of consolidation to copy. The next day a rumor to the effect that the American Union was to absorb the Western Union appeared on the first page of every New York newspaper. Edward knew exactly whence this rumor emanated. He had heard it talked over. Again, Western Union stock dropped several points. Then he noticed that Mr. Gould became a heavy buyer. So became Edward—as heavy as he could. Jay Gould pooh-poohed the latest rumor. The boy awaited developments.

On Sunday afternoon, Edward's Sunday-school teacher asked the boy to walk home with him, and on reaching the house took him into the study and asked him whether he felt justified in putting all his savings in Western Union just at that time when the price was tumbling so fast and the market was so unsteady. Edward assured his teacher that he was right, although he explained that he could not disclose the basis of his assurance.

Edward thought his teacher looked worried, and after a little there came the revelation that he, seeing that Edward was buying to his limit, had likewise done so. But the broker had bought on margin, and had his margin wiped out by the decline in the stock caused by the rumors. He explained to Edward that he could recoup his losses, heavy though they were—in fact, he explained that nearly everything he possessed was involved—if Edward's basis was sure and the stock would rcover.

Edward keenly felt the responsibility placed upon him.

He could never clearly diagnose his feelings when he saw his teacher in this new light. The broker's "customers" had been hinted at, and the boy of eighteen wondered how far his responsibility went, and how many persons were involved. But the deal came out all right, for when, three days afterward, the contract was made public, Western Union, of course, skyrocketed, Jay Gould sold out, Edward sold out, the teacher-broker sold out, and all the customers sold out!

How long a string it was Edward never discovered, but he determined there and then to end his Wall Street experience; his original amount had multiplied; he was content to let well enough alone, and from that day to this Edward Bok has kept out of Wall Street. He had seen enough of its manipulations; and, although on "the inside," he decided that the combination of his teacher and his customers was a responsibility too great for him to carry.

Furthermore, Edward decided to leave the Western Union. The longer he remained, the less he liked its atmosphere. And the closer his contact with Jay Gould the more doubtful he became of the wisdom of such an association and perhaps its unconscious influence upon his own life in its formative period.

In fact, it was an experience with Mr. Gould that definitely fixed Edward's determination. The financier decided one Saturday to leave on a railroad inspection tour on the following Monday. It was necessary that a special meeting of one of his railroad interests should be held before his departure, and he fixed the meeting for Sunday at eleven-thirty at his residence on Fifth Avenue. He asked Edward to be there to take the notes of the meeting.

The meeting was protracted, and at one o'clock Mr. Gould suggested an adjournment for luncheon, the meeting to reconvene at two. Turning to Edward, the financier said: "You may go out to luncheon and return in an hour." So, on Sunday afternoon, with the Windsor Hotel on the opposite corner as the only visible place to get something to eat, but where he could not afford to go, Edward, with just fifteen cents in his pocket, was turned out to find a luncheon place.

He bought three apples for five cents—all that he could afford to spend, and even this meant that he must walk home from the ferry to his house in Brooklyn—and these he ate as he walked up and down Fifth Avenue until his hour was over. When the meeting ended at three o'clock, Mr. Gould said that, as he was leaving for the West early next morning, he would like Edward to write out his notes, and have them at his house by eight o'clock. There were over forty note-book pages of minutes. The remainder of Edward's Sunday afternoon and evening was spent in transcribing the notes. By rising at half past five the next morning he reached Mr. Gould's house at a quarter to eight, handed him the minutes, and was dismissed without so much as a word of thanks or a nod of approval from the financier.

Edward felt that this exceeded the limit of fair treatment by employer of employee. He spoke of it to Mr. Cary, and asked whether he would object if he tried to get away from such influence and secure another position. His employer asked the boy in which direction he would like to go, and Edward unhesitatingly suggested the publishing business. He talked it over from every angle with his employer, and Mr. Cary not only agreed with him that his decision was wise, but promised to find him a position such as he had in mind.

It was not long before Mr. Cary made good his word,

and told Edward that his friend Henry Holt, the publisher, would like to give him a trial.

The day before he was to leave the Western Union Telegraph Company the fact of his resignation became known to Mr. Gould. The financier told the boy there was no reason for his leaving, and that he would personally see to it that a substantial increase was made in his salary. Edward explained that the salary, while of importance to him, did not influence him so much as securing a position in a business in which he felt he would be happier.

"And what business is that?" asked the financier.

"The publishing of books," replied the boy.

"You are making a great mistake," answered the little man, fixing his keen gray eyes on the boy. "Books are a luxury. The public spends its largest money on necessities: on what it can't do without. It must telegraph; it need not read. It can read in libraries. A promising boy such as you are, with his life before him, should choose the right sort of business, not the wrong one."

But, as facts proved, the "little wizard of Wall Street" was wrong in his prediction; Edward Bok was not choosing the wrong business.

Years afterward when Edward was cruising up the Hudson with a yachting party one Saturday afternoon, the sight of Jay Gould's mansion, upon approaching Irvington, awakened the desire of the women on board to see his wonderful orchid collection. Edward explained his previous association with the financier and offered to recall himself to him, if the party wished to take the chance of recognition. A note was written to Mr. Gould, and sent ashore, and the answer came back that they were welcome to visit the orchid houses. Jay Gould, in person, received the party, and, placing it under the personal conduct of his gardener, turned to Edward and, indicating a bench, said: "Come and sit down here with me."

"Well," said the financier, who was in his domestic mood, quite different from his Wall Street aspect, "I see in the papers that you seem to be making your way in the publishing business."

Edward expressed surprise that the Wall Street magnate had followed his work.

"I have because I always felt you had it in you to make a successful man. But not in that business," he added quickly. "You were born for the Street. You would have made a great success there, and that is what I had in mind for you. In the publishing business you will go just so far; in the Street you could have gone as far as you liked. There is room there; there is none in the publishing business. It's not too late now, for that matter," continued the "little wizard," fastening his steel eyes on the young man beside him!

And Edward Bok has often speculated whither Jay Gould might have led him. To many a young man, a suggestion from such a source would have seemed the one to heed and follow. But Edward Bok's instinct never failed him. He felt that his path lay far apart from that of Jay Gould—and the farther the better!

In 1882 Edward, with a feeling of distinct relief, left the employ of the Western Union Telegraph Company and associated himself with the publishing business in which he had correctly divined that his future lay.

His chief regret on leaving his position was in severing the close relations, almost as of father and son, between Mr. Cary and himself. When Edward was left alone, with the passing away of his father, Clarence Cary had put his sheltering arm around the lonely boy, and with the tremendous encouragement of the phrase that the boy never forgot, "I think you have it in you, Edward, to make a successful man," he took him under his wing. It was a turning-point in Edward Bok's life, as he felt at the time and as he saw more clearly afterward.

He remained in touch with his friend, however, keeping him advised of his progress in everything he did, not only at that time, but all through his later years. And it was given to Edward to feel the deep satisfaction of having Mr. Cary say, before he passed away, that the boy had more than justified the confidence reposed in him. Mr. Cary lived to see him well on his way, until, indeed, Edward had had the proud happiness of introducing to his benefactor the son who bore his name, Cary William Bok.

CHAPTER VIII

STARTING A NEWSPAPER SYNDICATE

Edward felt that his daytime hours, spent in a publishing atmosphere as stenographer with Henry Holt and Company, were more in line with his editorial duties during the evenings. *The Brooklyn Magazine* was soon earning a comfortable income for its two young proprietors, and their backers were entirely satisfied with the way it was being conducted. In fact, one of these backers, Mr. Rufus T. Bush, associated with the Standard Oil Company, who became especially interested, thought he saw in the success of the magazine a possible opening for one of his sons, who was shortly to be graduated from college. He talked to the publisher and editor about the idea, but the boys showed by their books that while there was a reasonable income for them, not wholly dependent on the magazine, there was no room for a third.

Mr. Bush now suggested that he buy the magazine for his son, alter its name, enlarge its scope, and make of it a national periodical. Arrangements were concluded, those who had financially backed the venture were fully paid, and the two boys received a satisfactory amount for their work in building up the magazine. Mr. Bush asked Edward to suggest a name for the new periodical, and in the following month of May, 1887, *The Brooklyn Magazine* became *The American Magazine,* with its publication office in New York. But, though a great deal of money was spent on the new magazine, it did not succeed. Mr. Bush sold his interest in the periodical, which, once more changing its name, became *The Cosmopolitan Magazine*. Since then it has passed through the hands of several owners, but the name has remained the same. Before Mr. Bush sold *The American Magazine* he had urged Edward to come back to it as its editor, with promise of financial support; but the young man felt instinctively that his return would not be wise. The magazine had been *The Cosmopolitan* only a short time when the new owners, Mr. Paul J. Slicht and Mr. E. D. Walker, also solicited the previous editor to accept reappointment. But Edward, feeling that his baby had been rechristened too often for him to father it again, declined the proposition. He had not heard the last of it, however, for, by a curious coincidence, its subsequent owner, entirely ignorant of Edward's previous association with the magazine, invited him to connect himself with it. Thus three times could Edward Bok have returned to the magazine for whose creation he was responsible.

Edward was now without editorial cares; but he had already, even before disposing of the magazine, embarked on another line of endeavor. In sending to a number of newspapers the advance sheets of a particularly striking "feature" in one of his numbers of *The Brooklyn Magazine*, it occurred to him that he was furnishing a good deal of valuable material to these papers without cost. It is true his magazine was receiving the advertising value of editorial comment; but he wondered whether the newspapers would not be willing to pay for the privilege of simultaneous publication. An inquiry or two proved that they would. Thus Edward stumbled upon the "syndicate" plan of furnishing the same article to a group of newspapers, one in each city, for simultaneous publication. He looked over the ground, and found that while his idea was not a new one, since two "syndicate" agencies already existed, the field was by no means fully covered, and that the success of a third agency would depend entirely upon its ability to furnish the newspapers with material equally good or better than they received from the others. After following the material furnished by these agencies for two or three weeks, Edward decided that there was plenty of room for his new ideas.

He discussed the matter with his former magazine partner, Colver, and suggested that if they could induce Mr. Beecher to write a weekly comment on current events for the newspapers it would make an auspicious beginning. They decided to talk it over with the famous preacher. For to be a "Plymouth boy"—that is, to go to the Plymouth Church Sunday-school and to attend church there—was to know personally and become devoted to Henry Ward Beecher. And the two were synonymous. There was no distance between Mr. Beecher and his "Plymouth boys." Each understood the other. The tie was that of absolute comradeship.

"I don't believe in it, boys," said Mr. Beecher when Edward and his friend broached the syndicate letter to him. "No one yet ever made a cent out of my supposed literary work."

All the more reason, was the argument, why some one should.

Mr. Beecher smiled! How well he knew the youthful enthusiasm that rushes in, etc.

"Well, all right! I like your pluck," he finally said. "I'll help you if I can."

The young editors agreed to pay Mr. Beecher a weekly sum of two hundred and fifty dollars—which he knew was considerable for them.

When the first article had been written they took him their first check. He looked at it quizzically, and then at the boys. Then he said simply: "Thank you." He took a pin and pinned the check to his desk. There it remained, much to their curiosity.

The following week he had written the second article and the boys gave him another check. He pinned that up over the other. "I like to look at them," was his only explanation, as he saw Edward's inquiring glance one morning.

The third check was treated the same way. When they handed him the fourth, one morning, as he was pinning it up over the others, he asked: "When do you get your money from the newspapers?"

He was told that the bills were going out that morning for the four letters constituting a month's service.

"I see," he remarked.

A fortnight passed, then one day Mr. Beecher asked: "Well, how are the checks coming in?"

"Very well," he was assured.

"Suppose you let me see how much you've got in," he suggested, and the boys brought the accounts to him.

After looking at them he said: "That's very interesting. How much have you in the bank?"

He was told the balance, less the checks given to him. "But I haven't turned them in yet," he explained. "Anyhow, you have enough in bank to meet the checks you have given me, and a profit besides, haven't you?"

He was assured they had.

Then, taking his bank-book from a drawer, he unpinned the six checks on his desk, indorsed each, wrote a deposit-slip, and, handing the book to Edward, said:

"Just hand that in at the bank as you go by, will you?"

Edward was very young then, and Mr. Beecher's methods of financiering seemed to him quite in line with current notions of the Plymouth pastor's lack of business knowledge. But as the years rolled on the incident appeared in a new light—a striking example of the great preacher's wonderful considerateness.

Edward had offered to help Mr. Beecher with his correspondence; at the close of one afternoon, while he was with the Plymouth pastor at work, an organ-grinder and a little girl came under the study window. A cold, driving rain was pelting down. In a moment Mr. Beecher noticed the girl's bare toes sticking out of her worn shoes.

He got up, went into the hall, and called for one of his granddaughters.

"Got any good, strong rain boots?" he asked when she appeared.

"Why, yes, grandfather. Why?" was the answer.

"More than one pair?" Mr. Beecher asked.

"Yes, two or three, I think."

"Bring me your strongest pair, will you, dear?" he asked. And as the girl looked at him with surprise he said: "Just one of my notions."

"Now, just bring that child into the house and put them on her feet for me, will you?" he said when the shoes came. "I'll be able to work so much better."

One rainy day, as Edward was coming up from Fulton Ferry with Mr. Beecher, they met an old woman soaked with the rain. "Here, you take this, my good woman," said the clergyman, putting his umbrella over her head and thrusting the handle into the astonished woman's hand. "Let's get into this," he said to Edward simply, as he hailed a passing car.

"There is a good deal of fraud about beggars," he remarked as he waved a sot away from him one day; "but that doesn't apply to women and children," he added; and he never passed such mendicants without stopping. All the stories about their being tools in the hands of accomplices failed to convince him. "They're women and children," he would say, and that settled it for him.

"What's the matter, son? Stuck?" he said once to a newsboy who was crying with a heavy bundle of papers under his arm.

"Come along with me, then," said Mr. Beecher, taking the boy's hand and leading him into the newspaper office a few doors up the street.

"This boy is stuck," he simply said to the man behind the counter. "Guess *The Eagle* can stand it better than this boy; don't you think so?"

To the grown man Mr. Beecher rarely gave charity. He believed in a return for his alms.

"Why don't you go to work?" he asked of a man who approached him one day in the street.

"Can't find any," said the man.

"Looked hard for it?" was the next question.

"I have," and the man looked Mr. Beecher in the eye.

"Want some?" asked Mr. Beecher.

"I do," said the man.

"Come with me," said the preacher. And then to Edward, as they walked along with the man following behind, he added: "That man is honest."

"Let this man sweep out the church," he said to the sexton when they had reached Plymouth Church.

"But, Mr. Beecher," replied the sexton with wounded pride, "it doesn't need it."

"Don't tell him so, though," said Mr. Beecher with a merry twinkle of the eye; and the sexton understood.

Mr. Beecher was constantly thoughtful of a struggling young man's welfare, even at the expense of his own material comfort. Anxious to save him from the labor of writing out the newspaper articles, Edward, himself employed during the daylight hours which Mr. Beecher preferred for his original work, suggested a stenographer. The idea appealed to Mr. Beecher, for he was very busy just then. He hesitated, but as Edward persisted, he said: "All right; let him come to-morrow."

The next day he said: "I asked that stenographer friend of yours not to come again. No use of my trying to dictate. I am too old to learn new tricks. Much easier for me to write myself."

Shortly after that, however, Mr. Beecher dictated to Edward some material for a book he was writing. Edward naturally wondered at this, and asked the stenographer what had happened.

"Nothing," he said. "Only Mr. Beecher asked me how much it would cost you to have me come to him each week. I told him, and then he sent me away."

That was Henry Ward Beecher!

Edward Bok was in the formative period between boyhood and young manhood when impressions meant lessons, and associations meant ideals. Mr. Beecher never disappointed. The closer one got to him, the greater he became—in striking contrast to most public men, as Edward had already learned.

Then, his interests and sympathies were enormously wide. He took in so much! One day Edward was walking past Fulton Market, in New York City, with Mr. Beecher.

"Never skirt a market," the latter said; "always go

through it. It's the next best thing, in the winter, to going South."

Of course all the marketmen knew him, and they knew, too, his love for green things.

"What do you think of these apples, Mr. Beecher?" one marketman would stop to ask.

Mr. Beecher would answer heartily: "Fine! Don't see how you grow them. All that my trees bear is a crop of scale. Still, the blossoms are beautiful in the spring, and I like an apple-leaf. Ever examine one?" The marketman never had. "Well, now, do, the next time you come across an apple-tree in the spring."

And thus he would spread abroad an interest in the beauties of nature which were commonly passed over.

"Wonderful man, Beecher is," said a market dealer in green goods once. "I had handled thousands of bunches of celery in my life and never noticed how beautiful its top leaves were until he picked up a bunch once and told me all about it. Now I haven't the heart to cut the leaves off when a customer asks me."

His idea of his own vegetable-gardening at Boscobel, his Peekskill home, was very amusing. One day Edward was having a hurried dinner, preparatory to catching the New York train. Mr. Beecher sat beside the boy, telling him of some things he wished done in Brooklyn.

"No, I thank you," said Edward, as the maid offered him some potatoes.

"Look here, young man," said Mr. Beecher, "don't pass those potatoes so lightly. They're of my own raising—and I reckon they cost me about a dollar a piece," he added with a twinkle in his eye.

He was an education in so many ways! One instance taught Edward the great danger of passionate speech that might unconsciously wound, and the manliness of instant recognition of the error. Swayed by an occasion, or by the responsiveness of an audience, Mr. Beecher would sometimes say something which was not meant as it sounded. One evening, at a great political meeting at Cooper Union, Mr. Beecher was at his brightest and wittiest. In the course of his remarks he had occasion to refer to ex-President Hayes; some one in the audience called out: "He was a softy!"

"No," was Mr. Beecher's quick response. "The country needed a poultice at that time, and got it."

"He's dead now, anyhow," responded the voice.

"Not dead, my friend: he only sleepeth."

It convulsed the audience, of course, and the reporters took it down in their books.

After the meeting Edward drove home with Mr. Beecher. After a while he asked: "Well, how do you think it went?"

Edward replied he thought it went very well, except that he did not like the reference to ex-President Hayes.

"What reference? What did I say?"

Edward repeated it.

"Did I say that?" he asked. Edward looked at him. Mr. Beecher's face was tense. After a few moments he said: "That's generally the way with extemporaneous remarks: they are always dangerous. The best impromptu speeches and remarks are the carefully prepared kind," he added.

Edward told him he regretted the reference because he knew that General Hayes would read it in the New York papers, and he would be nonplussed to understand it, considering the cordial relations which existed between the two men. Mr. Beecher knew of Edward's relations with the ex-President, and they had often talked of him together.

Nothing more was said of the incident. When the Beecher home was reached Mr. Beecher said: "Just come in a minute." He went straight to his desk, and wrote and wrote. It seemed as if he would never stop. At last he handed Edward an eight-page letter, closely written, addressed to General Hayes.

"Read that, and mail it, please, on your way home. Then it'll get there just as quickly as the New York papers will."

It was a superbly fine letter,—one of those letters which only Henry Ward Beecher could write in his tenderest moods. And the reply which came from Fremont, Ohio, was no less fine!

CHAPTER IX

THE FIRST "WOMAN'S PAGE," "LITERARY LEAVES,"
AND ENTERING SCRIBNER'S

Edward had been in the employ of Henry Holt and
Company as clerk and stenographer for two years when
Mr. Cary sent for him and told him that there was an opening in the publishing house of Charles Scribner's Sons, if
he wanted to make a change. Edward saw at once the
larger opportunities possible in a house of the importance
of the Scribners, and he immediately placed himself in
communication with Mr. Charles Scribner, with the result
that in January, 1884, he entered the employ of these
publishers as stenographer to the two members of the firm
and to Mr. Edward L. Burlingame, literary adviser to the
house. He was to receive a salary of eighteen dollars and
thirty-three cents per week, which was then considered a
fair wage for stenographic work. The typewriter had at
that time not come into use, and all letters were written
in long-hand. Once more his legible handwriting had secured for him a position.

Edward Bok was now twenty-one years of age. He
had already done a prodigious amount of work for his
years. He was always busy. Every spare moment of
his evenings was devoted either to writing his literary
letter, to the steady acquirement of autograph letters in
which he still persisted, or to helping Mr. Beecher in his
literary work. The Plymouth pastor was particularly
pleased with Edward's successful exploitation of his pen
work; and he afterward wrote: "Bok is the only man who

ever seemed to make my literary work go and get money out of it."

Enterprise and energy the boy unquestionably possessed, but one need only think back even thus far in his life to see the continuous good fortune which had followed him in the friendships he had made, and in the men with whom his life, at its most formative period, had come into close contact. If we are inclined to credit young Bok with an ever-willingness to work and a certain quality of initiative, the influences which played upon him must also be taken into account.

Take, for example, the peculiarly fortuitous circumstances under which he entered the Scribner publishing house. As stenographer to the two members of the firm, Bok was immediately brought into touch with the leading authors of the day, their works as they were discussed in the correspondence dictated to him, and the authors' terms upon which books were published. In fact, he was given as close an insight as it was possible for a young man to get into the inner workings of one of the large publishing houses in the United States, with a list peculiarly noted for the distinction of its authors and the broad scope of its books.

The Scribners had the foremost theological list of all the publishing houses; its educational list was exceptionally strong; its musical list excelled; its fiction represented the leading writers of the day; its general list was particularly noteworthy; and its foreign department, importing the leading books brought out in Great Britain and Europe, was an outstanding feature of the business. The correspondence dictated to Bok covered, naturally, all these fields, and a more remarkable opportunity for self-education was never offered a stenographer.

Mr. Burlingame was known in the publishing world for his singularly keen literary appreciation, and was accepted as one of the best judges of good fiction. Bok entered the Scribner employ as Mr. Burlingame was selecting the best short stories published within a decade for a set of books to be called "Short Stories by American Authors." The correspondence for this series was dictated to Bok, and he decided to read after Mr. Burlingame and thus get an idea of the best fiction of the day. So whenever his chief wrote to an author asking for permission to include his story in the proposed series, Bok immediately hunted up the story and read it.

Later, when the house decided to start *Scribner's Magazine*, and Mr. Burlingame was selected to be its editor, all the preliminary correspondence was dictated to Bok through his employers, and he received a first-hand education in the setting up of the machinery necessary for the publication of a magazine. All this he eagerly absorbed.

He was again fortunate in that his desk was placed in the advertising department of the house; and here he found, as manager, an old-time Brooklyn boy friend with whom he had gone to school, Frank N. Doubleday, to-day the senior partner of Doubleday, Page and Company. Bok had been attracted to advertising through his theatre programme and *Brooklyn Magazine* experience, and here was presented a chance to learn the art at first hand and according to the best traditions. So, whenever his stenographic work permitted, he assisted Mr. Doubleday in preparing and placing the advertisements of the books of the house.

Mr. Doubleday was just reviving the publication of a house-organ called *The Book Buyer*, and, given a chance to help in this, Bok felt he was getting back into the periodical field, especially since, under Mr. Doubleday's guidance, the little monthly soon developed into a literary magazine of very respectable size and generally bookish contents.

The house also issued another periodical, *The Presbyterian Review*, a quarterly under the editorship of a board of professors connected with the Princeton and Union Theological Seminaries. This ponderous-looking magazine was not composed of what one might call "light reading," and as the price of a single copy was eighty cents, and the advertisements it could reasonably expect were necessarily limited in number, the periodical was rather difficult to move. Thus the whole situation at the Scribners' was adapted to give Edward an all-round training in the publishing business. It was an exceptional opportunity.

He worked early and late. An increase in his salary soon told him that he was satisfying his employers, and then, when the new *Scribner's Magazine* appeared, and a little later Mr. Doubleday was delegated to take charge of the business end of it, Bok himself was placed in charge of the advertising department, with the publishing details of the two periodicals on his hands.

He suddenly found himself directing a stenographer instead of being a stenographer himself. Evidently his apprentice days were over. He had, in addition, the charge of sending all the editorial copies of the new books to the press for review, and of keeping a record of those reviews. This naturally brought to his desk the authors of the house who wished to see how the press received their works.

The study of the writers who were interested in following the press notices of their books, and those who were indifferent to them became a fascinating game to young Bok. He soon discovered that the greater the author the less he seemed to care about his books once they were published. Bok noticed this, particularly, in the case of Robert Louis Stevenson, whose work had attracted him, but, although he used the most subtle means to inveigle the author into the office to read the press notices, he never succeeded. Stevenson never seemed to have the slightest interest in what the press said of his books.

One day Mr. Burlingame asked Bok to take some proofs to Stevenson at his home; thinking it might be a propitious moment to interest the author in the popular acclaim that followed the publication of *Doctor Jekyll and Mr. Hyde*, Bok put a bunch of press notices in his pocket. He found the author in bed, smoking his inevitable cigarette.

As the proofs were to be brought back, Bok waited, and thus had an opportunity for nearly two hours to see the author at work. No man ever went over his proofs more carefully than did Stevenson; his corrections were numerous; and sometimes for ten minutes at a time he would sit smoking and thinking over a single sentence, which, when he had satisfactorily shaped it in his mind, he would recast on the proof.

Stevenson was not a prepossessing figure at these times. With his sallow skin and his black dishevelled hair, with finger-nails which had been allowed to grow very long, with fingers discolored by tobacco—in short, with a general untidiness that was all his own, Stevenson, so Bok felt, was an author whom it was better to read than to see. And yet his kindliness and gentleness more than offset the unattractiveness of his physical appearance.

After one or two visits from Bok, having grown accustomed to him, Stevenson would discuss some sentence in an article, or read some amended paragraph out loud and ask whether Bok though it sounded better. To pass upon Stevenson as a stylist was, of course, hardly within Bok's mental reach, so he kept discreetly silent when Stevenson asked his opinion.

In fact, Bok reasoned it out that the novelist did not really expect an answer or an opinion, but was at such times thinking aloud. The mental process, however, was immensely interesting, particularly when Stevenson would ask Bok to hand him a book on words lying on an adjacent table. "So hard to find just the right word," Stevenson would say, and Bok got his first realization of the truth of the maxim: "Easy writing, hard reading; hard writing, easy reading."

On this particular occasion when Stevenson finished, Bok pulled out his clippings, told the author how his book was being received, and was selling, what the house was doing to advertise it, explained the forthcoming play by Richard Mansfield, and then offered the press notices.

Stevenson took the bundle and held it in his hand.

"That's very nice to tell me all you have," he said, "and I have been greatly interested. But you have really told me all about it, haven't you, so why should I read these notices? Hadn't I better get busy on another paper for Mr. Burlingame for the next magazine, else he'll be after me? You know how impatient these editors are." And he handed back the notices.

Bok saw it was of no use: Stevenson was interested in his work, but, beyond a certain point, not in the world's reception of it. Bok's estimate of the author rose immeasurably. His attitude was in such sharp contrast to that of others who came almost daily into the office to see what the papers said, often causing discomfiture to the young advertising director by insisting upon taking the notices with them. But Bok always countered this desire by reminding the author that, of course, in that case he could not quote from these desirable notices in his advertisements of the book. And, invariably, the notices were left behind!

It now fell to the lot of the young advertiser to arouse the interest of the public in what were to be some of the most widely read and best-known books of the day: Robert Louis Stevenson's *Dr. Jekyll and Mr. Hyde*; Frances Hodgson Burnett's *Little Lord Fauntleroy*; Andrew Carnegie's *Triumphant Democracy*; Frank R. Stockton's *The Lady, or the Tiger?* and his *Rudder Grange*, and a succession of other books.

The advertising of these books keenly sharpened the publicity sense of the developing advertising director. One book could best be advertised by the conventional means of the display advertisement; another, like *Triumphant Democracy*, was best served by sending out to the newspapers a "broadside" of pungent extracts; public curiosity in a story like *The Lady, or the Tiger?* was, of course, whetted by the publication of literary notes as to the real dénouement the author had in mind in writing the story. Whenever Mr. Stockton came into the office Bok pumped him dry as to his experiences with the story, such as when, at a dinner party, his hostess served an ice-cream lady and a tiger to the author, and the whole company watched which he chose.

"And which did you choose?" asked the advertising director.

"*Et tu, Brute?*" Stockton smilingly replied. "Well, I'll tell you. I asked the butler to bring me another spoon, and then, with a spoon in each hand, I attacked both the lady and the tiger at the same time."

Once, when Stockton was going to Boston by the night boat, every room was taken. The ticket agent recognized the author, and promised to get him a desirable room if the author would tell which he had had in mind, the lady or the tiger.

"Produce the room," answered Stockton.

The man did. Stockton paid for it, and then said: "To tell you the truth, my friend, I don't know."

And that *was* the truth, as Mr. Stockton confessed to his friends. The idea of the story had fascinated him; when he began it he purposed to give it a definite ending. But when he reached the end he didn't know himself which to produce out of the open door, the lady or the tiger, "and so," he used to explain, "I made up my mind to leave it hanging in the air."

When the stories of *Dr. Jekyll and Mr. Hyde* and *Little Lord Fauntleroy* were made into plays, Bok was given an opportunity for an entirely different kind of publicity. Both plays were highly successful; they ran for weeks in succession, and each evening Bok had circulars of the books in every seat of the theatre; he had a table filled with the books in the foyer of each theatre; and he bombarded the newspapers with stories of Mr. Mansfield's method of making the quick change from one character to the other in the dual rôle of the Stevenson play, and with anecdotes about the boy Tommy Russell in Mrs. Burnett's play. The sale of the books went merrily on, and kept pace with the success of the plays. And it all sharpened the initiative of the young advertiser and developed his sense for publicity.

One day while waiting in the anteroom of a publishing

house to see a member of the firm, he picked up a book and began to read it. Since he had to wait for nearly an hour, he had read a large part of the volume when he was at last admitted to the private office. When his business was finished, Bok asked the publisher why this book was not selling.

"I don't know," replied the publisher. "We had great hopes for it, but somehow or other the public has not responded to it."

"Are you sure you are telling the public about it in the right way?" ventured Bok.

The Scribner advertising had by this time attracted the attention of the publishing world, and this publisher was entirely ready to listen to a suggestion from his youthful caller.

"I wish we published it," said Bok. "I think I could make it a go. It's all in the book."

"How would you advertise it?" asked the publisher.

Bok promised the publisher he would let him know. He carried with him a copy of the book, wrote some advertisements for it, prepared an attractive "broadside" of extracts, to which the book easily lent itself, wrote some literary notes about it, and sent the whole collection to the publisher. Every particle of "copy" which Bok had prepared was used, the book began to sell, and within three months it was the most discussed book of the day.

The book was Edward Bellamy's *Looking Backward*.

Meanwhile, Mr. Beecher's weekly newspaper "syndicate" letter was not only successful in itself, it made liberal money for the writer and for its two young publishers, but it served to introduce Edward Bok's proposed agency to the newspapers under the most favorable conditions. With one stroke, the attention of newspaper editors had been attracted, and Edward concluded to take quick advantage of it. He organized the Bok Syndicate Press, with offices in New York, and his brother, William J. Bok, as partner and active manager.

Edward's attention was now turned, for the first time, to women and their reading habits. He became interested in the fact that the American woman was not a newspaper reader. He tried to find out the psychology of this, and finally reached the conclusion, on looking over the newspapers, that the absence of any distinctive material for women was a factor. He talked the matter over with several prominent New York editors, who frankly acknowledged that they would like nothing better than to interest women, and make them readers of their papers. But they were equally frank in confessing that they were ignorant both of what women wanted, and, even if they knew, of where such material was to be had. Edward at once saw that here was an open field. It was a productive field, since, as woman was the purchasing power, it would benefit the newspaper enormously in its advertising if it could offer a feminine clientele.

There was a bright letter of New York gossip published in the *New York Star*, called "Bab's Babble." Edward had read it, and saw the possibility of syndicating this item as a woman's letter from New York. He instinctively realized that women all over the country would read it. He sought out the author, made arrangements with her and with former Governor Dorscheimer, owner of the paper, and the letter was sent out to a group of papers. It was an instantaneous success, and a syndicate of ninety newspapers was quickly organized.

Edward followed this up by engaging Ella Wheeler

Wilcox, then at the height of her career, to write a weekly
letter on women's topics.   This he syndicated in conjunction with the other letter, and the editors invariably grouped
the two letters.   This, in turn, naturally led to the idea of
supplying an entire page of matter of interest to women.
The plan was proposed to a number of editors, who at once
saw the possibilities in it and promised support.   The young
syndicator now laid under contribution all the famous
women writers of the day; he chose the best of the men
writers to write on women's topics; and it was not long
before the syndicate was supplying a page of women's
material.   The newspapers played up the innovation, and
thus was introduced into the newspaper press of the United
States the "Woman's Page."

The material supplied by the Bok Syndicate Press was
of the best; the standard was kept high; the writers were
selected from among the most popular authors of the day;
and readability was the cardinal note.   The women bought
the newspapers containing the new page, the advertiser
began to feel the presence of the new reader, and every
newspaper that could not get the rights for the "Bok Page,"
as it came to be known, started a "Woman's Page" of its
own.   Naturally, the material so obtained was of an in-
ferior character.   No single newspaper could afford what
the syndicate, with the expense divided among a hundred
newspapers, could pay.   Nor had the editors of these woman's pages either a standard or a policy.   In desperation
they engaged any person they could to "get a lot of woman's stuff."   It *was* stuff, and of the trashiest kind.   So
that almost coincident with the birth of the idea began its
abuse and disintegration; the result we see in the meaningless presentations which pass for "woman's pages" in
the newspaper of to-day.

This is true even of the woman's material in the leading newspapers, and the reason is not difficult to find. The average editor has, as a rule, no time to study the changing conditions of women's interests; his time is and must be engrossed by the news and editorial pages. He usually delegates the Sunday "specials" to some editor who, again, has little time to study the everchanging women's problems, particularly in these days, and he relies upon unintelligent advice, or he places his "woman's page" in the hands of some woman with the comfortable assurance that, being a woman, she ought to know what interests her sex.

But having given the subject little thought, he attaches minor importance to the woman's "stuff," regarding it rather in the light of something that he "must carry to catch the women"; and forthwith he either forgets it or refuses to give the editor of his woman's page even a reasonable allowance to spend on her material. The result is, of course, inevitable: pages of worthless material. There is, in fact, no part of the Sunday newspaper of to-day upon which so much good and now expensive white paper is wasted as upon the pages marked for the home, for women, and for children.

Edward Bok now became convinced, from his book-publishing association, that if the American women were not reading the newspapers, the American public, as a whole, was not reading the number of books that it should, considering the intelligence and wealth of the people, and the cheap prices at which books were sold. He concluded to see whether he could not induce the newspapers to give larger and more prominent space to the news of the book world.

Owing to his constant contact with authors, he was in

a peculiarly fortunate position to know their plans in advance of execution, and he was beginning to learn the ins and outs of the book-publishing world. He canvassed the newspapers subscribing to his syndicate features, but found a disinclination to give space to literary news. To the average editor, purely literary features held less of an appeal than did the features for women. Fewer persons were interested in books, they declared; besides, the publishing houses were not so liberal advertisers as the department stores. The whole question rested on a commercial basis.

Edward believed he could convince editors of the public interest in a newsy, readable New York literary letter, and he prevailed upon the editor of the *New York Star* to allow him to supplement the book reviews of George Parsons Lathrop in that paper by a column of literary chat called "Literary Leaves." For a number of weeks he continued to write this department, and confine it to the New York paper, feeling that he needed the experience for the acquirement of a readable style, and he wanted to be sure that he had opened a sufficient number of productive news channels to ensure a continuous flow of readable literary information.

Occasionally he sent to an editor here and there what he thought was a particularly newsy letter just "for his information, not for sale." The editor of the *Philadelphia Times* was the first to discover that his paper wanted the letter, and the *Boston Journal* followed suit. Then the editor of the *Cincinnati Times-Star* discovered the letter in the *New York Star*, and asked that it be supplied weekly with the letter. These newspapers renamed the letter "Bok's Literary Leaves," and the feature started on its successful career.

CHAPTER X

THE CHANCES FOR SUCCESS

Edward Bok does not now remember whether the mental picture had been given him, or whether he had conjured it up for himself; but he certainly was possessed of the idea, as are so many young men entering business, that the path which led to success was very difficult: that it was overfilled with a jostling, bustling, panting crowd, each eager to reach the goal; and all ready to dispute every step that a young man should take; and that favoritism only could bring one to the top.

After Bok had been in the world of affairs, he wondered where were these choked avenues, these struggling masses, these competitors for every inch of vantage. Then he gradually discovered that they did not exist.

In the first place, he found every avenue leading to success wide open and certainly not overpeopled. He was surprised how few there were who really stood in a young man's way. He found that favoritism was not the factor that he had been led to suppose. He realized it existed in a few isolated cases, but to these every one had pointed and about these every one had talked until, in the public mind, they had multiplied in number and assumed a proportion that the facts did not bear out.

Here and there a relative "played a favorite," but even with the push and influence behind him "the lucky one," as he was termed, did not seem to make progress, unless he had merit. It was not long before Bok discovered that the possession of sheer merit was the only real factor that actually counted in any of the places where he had been employed or in others which he had watched; that business was so constructed and conducted that nothing else, in the face of competition, could act as current coin. And the amazing part of it all to Bok was how little merit there was. Nothing astonished him more than the low average ability of those with whom he worked or came into contact.

He looked at the top, and instead of finding it over-crowded, he was surprised at the few who had reached there; the top fairly begged for more to climb its heights.

For every young man, earnest, eager to serve, willing to do more than he was paid for, he found ten trying to solve the problem of how little they could actually do for the pay received.

It interested Bok to listen to the talk of his fellow-workers during luncheon hours and at all other times outside of office hours. When the talk did turn on the business with which they were concerned, it consisted almost entirely of wages, and he soon found that, with scarcely an exception, every young man was terribly underpaid, and that his employer absolutely failed to appreciate his work. It was interesting, later, when Bok happened to get the angle of the employer, to discover that, invariably, these same lamenting young men were those who, from the employer's point of view, were either greatly overpaid or so entirely worthless as to be marked for early decapitation.

Bok felt that this constant thought of the wages earned or deserved was putting the cart before the horse; he had schooled himself into the belief that if he did his work well, and accomplished more than was expected of him, the question of wages would take care of itself. But, according to the talk on every side, it was he who had the cart before the horse. Bok had not only tried always to fill the particular job set for him, but had made it a rule at the same time to study the position just ahead, to see what it was like, what it demanded, and then, as the opportunity presented itself, do a part of that job in addition to his own. As a stenographer, he tried always to clear off the day's work before he closed his desk. This was not always possible, but he kept it before him as a rule to be followed rather than violated.

One morning Bok's employer happened to come to the office earlier than usual, to find the letters he had dictated late in the afternoon before lying on his desk ready to be signed.

"These are the letters I gave you late yesterday afternoon, are they not?" asked the employer.

"Yes, sir."

"Must have started early this morning, didn't you?"

"No, sir," answered Bok. "I wrote them out last evening before I left."

"Like to get your notes written out before they get stale?"

"Yes, sir."

"Good idea," said the employer.

"Yes, sir," answered Bok, "and I think it is even a better idea to get a day's work off before I take my apron off."

"Well said," answered the employer, and the following payday Bok found an increase in his weekly envelope.

It is only fair, however, to add here, parenthetically, that it is neither just nor considerate to a conscientious stenographer for an employer to delay his dictation until the end of the day's work, when, merely by judicious management of his affairs and time, he can give his dictation directly after opening his morning mail. There are two sides to every question; but sometimes the side of the stenographer is not kept in mind by the employer.

Bok found it a uniform rule among his fellow-workers to do exactly the opposite to his own idea; there was an astonishing unanimity in working by the clock; where the hour of closing was five o'clock the preparations began five minutes before, with the hat and overcoat over the back of the chair ready for the stroke of the hour. This concert of action was curiously universal, no "overtime" was ever to be thought of, and, as occasionally happened when the work did go over the hour, it was not, to use the mildest term, done with care, neatness, or accuracy; it was, to use a current phrase, "slammed off." Every moment beyond five o'clock in which the worker was asked to do anything was by just so much an imposition on the part of the employer, and so far as it could be safely shown, this impression was gotten over to him.

There was an entire unwillingness to let business interfere with any anticipated pleasure or personal engagement. The office was all right between nine and five; one had to be there to earn a living; but after five, it was not to be thought of for one moment. The elevators which ran on the stroke of five were never large enough to hold the throng which besieged them.

The talk during lunch hour rarely, if ever, turned toward business, except as said before, when it dealt with underpaid services. In the spring and summer it was invariably of baseball, and scores of young men knew the batting averages of the different players and the standing of the clubs with far greater accuracy than they knew the standing or the discounts of the customers of their

employers. In the winter the talk was all of dancing, box-
ing, or plays.

It soon became evident to Bok why scarcely five out
of every hundred of the young men whom he knew made
any business progress. They were not interested; it was a
case of a day's work and a day's pay; it was not a question
of how much one could do but how little one could get away
with. The thought of how well one might do a given thing
never seemed to occur to the average mind.

"Oh, what do you care?" was the favorite expression.
"The boss won't notice it if you break your back over
his work; you won't get any more pay."

And there the subject was dismissed, and thoroughly
dismissed, too.

Eventually, then, Bok learned that the path that led
to success was wide open: the competition was negligible.
There was no jostling. In fact, travel on it was just a trifle
lonely. One's fellow-travellers were excellent company, but
they were few! It was one of Edward Bok's greatest surprises, but it was also one of his greatest stimulants.
To go where others could not go, or were loath to go, where
at least they were not, had a tang that savored of the fresh-
est kind of adventure. And the way was so simple, so
much simpler, in fact, than its avoidance, which called
for so much argument, explanation, and discussion. One
had merely to do all that one could do, a little more than
one was asked or expected to do, and immediately one's
head rose above the crowd and one was in an employer's
eye—where it is always so satisfying for an employee to be!
And as so few heads lifted themselves above the many,
there was never any danger that they would not be seen.

Of course, Edward Bok had to prove to himself that
his conception of conditions was right. He felt instinctively

that it was, however, and with this stimulus he bucked the line hard. When others played, he worked, fully convinced that his play-time would come later. Where others shirked, he assumed. Where others lagged, he accelerated his pace. Where others were indifferent to things around them, he observed and put away the results for possible use later. He did not make of himself a pack-horse; what he undertook he did from interest in it, and that made it a pleasure to him when to others it was a burden. He instinctively reasoned it out that an unpleasant task is never accomplished by stepping aside from it, but that, unerringly, it will return later to be met and done.

Obstacles, to Edward Bok, soon became merely difficulties to be overcome, and he trusted to his instinct to show him the best way to overcome them. He soon learned that the hardest kind of work was back of every success; that nothing in the world of business just happened, but that everything was brought about, and only in one way—by a willingness of spirit and a determination to carry through. He soon exploded for himself the misleading and comfortable theory of luck: the only lucky people, he found, were those who worked hard. To them, luck came in the shape of what they had earned. There were exceptions here and there, as there are to every rule; but the majority of these, he soon found, were more in the seeming than in the reality. Generally speaking—and of course to this rule there are likewise exceptions, or as the Frenchman said, "All generalizations are false, including this one"—a man got in this world about what he worked for.

And that became, for himself, the rule of Edward Bok's life.

CHAPTER XI

From his boyhood days (up to the present writing) Bok was a pronounced baseball "fan," and there was, too, a baseball team among the Scribner young men of which he was a part. This team played, each Saturday afternoon, a team from another publishing house, and for two seasons it was unbeatable. Not only was this baseball aggregation close to the hearts of the Scribner employees, but, in an important game, the junior member of the firm played on it and the senior member was a spectator. Frank N. Doubleday played on first base; William D. Moffat, later of Moffat, Yard & Company, and now editor of *The Mentor*, was behind the bat; Bok pitched; Ernest Dressel North, the present authority on rare editions of books, was in the field, as were also Ray Safford, now a director in the Scribner corporation, and Owen W. Brewer, at present a prominent figure in Chicago's book world. It was a happy group, all closely banded together in their business interests and in their human relations as well.

With *Scribner's Magazine* now in the periodical field, Bok would be asked on his trips to the publishing houses to have an eye open for advertisements for that periodical as well. Hence his education in the solicitation of advertisements became general, and gave him a sympathetic understanding of the problems of the advertising solicitor which was to stand him in good stead when, in his later experience, he was called upon to view the business problems of a magazine from the editor's position.

His knowledge of the manufacture of the two magazines
in his charge was likewise educative, as was the fascinating study of typography which always had, and has to-
day, a wonderful attraction for him.

It was, however, in connection with the advertising
of the general books of the house, and in his relations
with their authors, that Bok found his greatest interest.
It was for him to find the best manner in which to introduce to the public the books issued by the house, and
the general study of the psychology of publicity which
this called for attracted Bok greatly.

Although the Scribners did not publish Mark Twain's
books, the humorist was a frequent visitor to the retail store,
and occasionally he would wander back to the publishing
department located at the rear of the store, which was then
at 743 Broadway.

Smoking was not permitted in the Scribner offices,
and, of course, Mark Twain was always smoking. He
generally smoked a granulated tobacco which he kept in
a long check bag made of silk and rubber. When he sauntered to the back of the Scribner store, he would generally
knock the residue from the bowl of the pipe, take out the
stem, place it in his vest pocket, like a pencil, and drop
the bowl into the bag containing the granulated tobacco.
When he wanted to smoke again (which was usually five
minutes later) he would fish out the bowl, now automatically
filled with tobacco, insert the stem, and strike a light.
One afternoon as he wandered into Bok's office, he was just
putting his pipe away. The pipe, of the corncob variety,
was very aged and black. Bok asked him whether it was
the only pipe he had.

"Oh, no," Mark answered, "I have several. But
they're all like this. I never smoke a new corncob pipe.

A new pipe irritates the throat. No corncob pipe is fit for anything until it has been used at least a fortnight."

"How do you break in a pipe, then?" asked Bok.

"That's the trick," answered Mark Twain. "I get a cheap man—a man who doesn't amount to much, anyhow: who would be as well, or better, dead—and pay him a dollar to break in the pipe for me. I get him to smoke the pipe for a couple of weeks, then put in a new stem, and continue operations as long as the pipe holds together."

Bok's newspaper syndicate work had brought him into contact with Fanny Davenport, then at the zenith of her career as an actress. Miss Davenport, or Mrs. Melbourne McDowell as she was in private life, had never written for print; but Bok, seeing that she had something to say about her art and the ability to say it, induced her to write for the newspapers through his syndicate. The actress was overjoyed to have revealed to her a hitherto unsuspected gift; Bok published her articles successfully, and gave her a publicity that her press agent had never dreamed of. Miss Davenport became interested in the young publisher, and after watching the methods which he employed in successfully publishing her writings, decided to try to obtain his services as her assistant manager. She broached the subject, offered him a five years' contract for forty weeks' service, with a minimum of fifteen weeks each year to spend in or near New York, at a salary, for the first year, of three thousand dollars, increasing annually until the fifth year, when he was to receive sixty-four hundred dollars.

Bok was attracted to the work: he had never seen the United States, was anxious to do so, and looked upon the chance as a good opportunity. Miss Davenport had the contract made out, executed it, and then, in high glee, Bok took it home to show it to his mother. He had reckoned without question upon her approval, only to meet with an immediate and decided negative to the proposition as a whole, general and specific. She argued that the theatrical business was not for him; and she saw ahead and pointed out so strongly the mistake he was making that he sought Miss Davenport the next day and told her of his mother's stand. The actress suggested that she see the mother; she did, that day, and she came away from the interview a wiser if a sadder woman. Miss Davenport frankly told Bok that with such an instinctive objection as his mother seemed to have, he was right to follow her advice and the contract was not to be thought of.

It is difficult to say whether this was or was not for Bok the turning-point which comes in the life of every young man. Where the venture into theatrical life would have led him no one can, of course, say. One thing is certain: Bok's instinct and reason both failed him in this instance. He believes now that had his venture into the theatrical field been temporary or permanent, the experiment, either way, would have been disastrous.

Looking back and viewing the theatrical profession even as it was in that day (of a much higher order than now), he is convinced he would never have been happy in it. He might have found this out in a year or more, after the novelty of travelling had worn off, and asked release from his contract; in that case he would have broken his line of progress in the publishing business. From whatever viewpoint he has looked back upon this, which he now believes to have been the crisis in his life, he is convinced that his mother's instinct saved him from a grievous mistake.

The Scribner house, in its foreign-book department, had imported some copies of Bourrienne's *Life of Napoleon*, and a set had found its way to Bok's desk for advertising purposes. He took the books home to glance them over, found himself interested, and sat up half the night to read them. Then he took the set to the editor of the *New York Star*, and suggested that such a book warranted a special review, and offered to leave the work for the literary editor.

"You have read the books?" asked the editor.

"Every word," returned Bok.

"Then, why don't you write the review?" suggested the editor.

This was a new thought to Bok. "Never wrote a review," he said.

"Try it," answered the editor. "Write a column."

"A column wouldn't scratch the surface of this book," suggested the embryo reviewer.

"Well, give it what it is worth," returned the editor.

Bok did. He wrote a page of the paper.

"Too much, too much," said the editor. "Heavens, man, we've got to get some news into this paper."

"Very well," returned the reviewer. "Read it, and cut it where you like. That's the way I see the book."

And next Sunday the review appeared, word for word, as Bok had written it. His first review had successfully passed!

But Bok was really happiest in that part of his work which concerned itself with the writing of advertisements. The science of advertisement writing, which meant to him the capacity to say much in little space, appealed strongly. He found himself more honestly attracted to this than to the writing of his literary letter, his editorials, or his book reviewing, of which he was now doing a good deal. He determined to follow where his bent led; he studied the mechanics of unusual advertisements wherever he saw them; he eagerly sought a knowledge of typography and its best

handling in an advertisement, and of the value and relation of illustrations to text. He perceived that his work
along these lines seemed to give satisfaction to his employers, since they placed more of it in his hands to do;
and he sought in every way to become proficient in the
art.

To publishers whose advertisements he secured for
the periodicals in his charge, he made suggestions for the
improvement of their announcements, and found his suggestions accepted. He early saw the value of white space
as one of the most effective factors in advertising; but this
was a difficult argument, he soon found, to convey successfully to others. A white space in an advertisement was
to the average publisher something to fill up; Bok saw
in it something to cherish for its effectiveness. But he
never got very far with his idea: he could not convince
(perhaps because he failed to express his ideas convincingly)
his advertisers of what he felt and believed so strongly.

An occasion came in which he was permitted to prove
his contention. The Scribners had published Andrew
Carnegie's volume, *Triumphant Democracy*, and the author
desired that some special advertising should be done in
addition to that allowed by the appropriation made by
the house. To Bok's grateful ears came the injunction
from the steel magnate: "Use plenty of white space."
In conjunction with Mr. Doubleday, Bok prepared and
issued this extra advertising, and for once, at least, the
wisdom of using white space was demonstrated. But it
was only a flash in the pan. Publishers were unwilling
to pay for "unused space," as they termed it. Each book
was a separate unit, others argued: it was not like advertising one article continuously in which money could be
invested; and only a limited amount could be spent on

a book which ran its course, even at its best, in a very short time.

And, rightly or wrongly, book advertising has continued much along the same lines until the present day. In fact, in no department of manufacturing or selling activity has there been so little progress during the past fifty years as in bringing books to the notice of the public. In all other lines, the producer has brought his wares to the public, making it easier and still easier for it to obtain his goods, while the public, if it wants a book, must still seek the book instead of being sought by it.

That there is a tremendous unsupplied book demand in this country there is no doubt: the wider distribution and easier access given to periodicals prove this point. Now and then there has been tried an unsupported or not well-thought-out plan for bringing books to a public not now reading them, but there seems little or no understanding of the fact that there lies an uncultivated field of tremendous promise to the publisher who will strike out on a new line and market his books, so that the public will not have to ferret out a book-store or wind through the maze of a department store. The American reading public is not the book-reading public that it should be or could be made to be; but the habit must be made easy for it to acquire. Books must be placed where the public can readily get at them. It will not, of its own volition, seek them. It did not do so with magazines; it will not do so with books.

In the meanwhile, Bok's literary letter had prospered until it was now published in some forty-five newspapers. One of these was the *Philadelphia Times*. In that paper, each week, the letter had been read by Mr. Cyrus H. K. Curtis, the owner and publisher of *The Ladies' Home Journal*. Mr. Curtis had decided that he needed an editor for his magazine, in order to relieve his wife, who was then editing it, and he fixed upon the writer of *Literary Leaves* as his man. He came to New York, consulted Will Carleton, the poet, and found that while the letter was signed by William J. Bok, it was actually written by his brother who was with the Scribners. So he sought Bok out there.

The publishing house had been advertising in the Philadelphia magazine, so that the visit of Mr. Curtis was not an occasion for surprise. Mr. Curtis told Bok he had read his literary letter in the *Philadelphia Times*, and suggested that perhaps he might write a similar department for *The Ladies' Home Journal*. Bok saw no reason why he should not, and told Mr. Curtis so, and promised to send over a trial instalment. The Philadelphia publisher then deftly went on, explained editorial conditions in his magazine, and, recognizing the ethics of the occasion by not offering Bok another position while he was already occupying one, asked him if he knew the man for the place.

"Are you talking at me or through me?" asked Bok.

"Both," replied Mr. Curtis.

This was in April of 1889.

Bok promised Mr. Curtis he would look over the field, and meanwhile he sent over to Philadelphia the promised trial "literary gossip" instalment. It pleased Mr. Curtis, who suggested a monthly department, to which Bok consented. He also turned over in his mind the wisdom of interrupting his line of progress with the Scribners, and in New York, and began to contemplate the possibilities in Philadelphia and the work there.

He gathered a collection of domestic magazines then published, and looked them over to see what was already

in the field. Then he began to study himself, his capacity
for the work, and the possibility of finding it congenial.
He realized that it was absolutely foreign to his Scribner
work: that it meant a radical departure. But his work with
his newspaper syndicate naturally occurred to him, and he
studied it with a view of its adaptation to the field of the
Philadelphia magazine.

His next step was to take into his confidence two or
three friends whose judgment he trusted and discuss the
possible change. Without an exception, they advised
against it. The periodical had no standing, they argued;
Bok would be out of sympathy with its general atmosphere after his Scribner environment; he was now in the
direct line of progress in New York publishing houses; and,
to cap the climax, they each argued in turn, he would be
buried in Philadelphia: New York was the centre, etc., etc.

More than any other single argument, this last point
destroyed Bok's faith in the judgment of his friends. He
had had experience enough to realize that a man could not
be buried in any city, provided he had the ability to stand
out from his fellow-men. He knew from his biographical
reading that cream will rise to the surface anywhere, in
Philadelphia as well as in New York: it all depended on
whether the cream was there: it was up to the man. Had
he within him that peculiar, subtle something that, for the
want of a better phrase, we call the editorial instinct?
That was all there was to it, and that decision had to be his
and his alone!

A business trip for the Scribners now calling him West,
Bok decided to stop at Philadelphia, have a talk with Mr.
Curtis, and look over his business plant. He did this, and
found Mr. Curtis even more desirous than before to have

him consider the position. Bok's instinct was strongly in favor of an acceptance. A natural impulse moved him, without reasoning, to action. Reasoning led only to a cautious mental state, and caution is a strong factor in the Dutch character. The longer he pursued a conscious process of reasoning, the farther he got from the position. But the instinct remained strong.

On his way back from the West, he stopped in Philadelphia again to consult his friend, George W. Childs; and here he found the only person who was ready to encourage him to make the change.

Bok now laid the matter before his mother, in whose feminine instinct he had supreme confidence. With her, he met with instant discouragement. But in subsequent talks he found that her opposition was based not upon the possibilities inherent in the position, but on a mother's natural disinclination to be separated from one of her sons. In the case of Fanny Davenport's offer the mother's instinct was strong against the proposition itself. But in the present instance it was the mother's love that was speaking; not her instinct or judgment.

Bok now consulted his business associates, and, to a man, they discouraged the step, but almost invariably upon the argument that it was suicidal to leave New York. He had now a glimpse of the truth that there is no man so provincially narrow as the untravelled New Yorker who believes in his heart that the sun rises in the East River and sets in the North River.

He realized more keenly than ever before that the decision rested with him alone. On September 1, 1889, Bok wrote to Mr. Curtis, accepting the position in Philadelphia; and on October 13 following he left the Scribners, where he had been so fortunate and so happy, and, after a week's vacation, followed where his instinct so strongly led, but where his reason wavered.

On October 20, 1889, Edward Bok became the editor of *The Ladies' Home Journal.*

CHAPTER XII

There is a popular notion that the editor of a woman's magazine should be a woman. At first thought, perhaps, this sounds logical. But it is a curious fact that by far the larger number of periodicals for women, the world over, are edited by men; and where, as in some cases, a woman is the proclaimed editor, the direction of the editorial policy is generally in the hands of a man, or group of men, in the background. Why this is so has never been explained, any more than why the majority of women's dressmakers are men; why music, with its larger appeal to women, has been and is still being composed, largely, by men, and why its greatest instrumental performers are likewise men; and why the church, with its larger membership of women, still has, as it always has had, men for its greatest preachers.

In fact, we may well ponder whether the full editorial authority and direction of a modern magazine, either essentially feminine in its appeal or not, can safely be entrusted to a woman when one considers how largely executive is the nature of such a position, and how thoroughly sensitive the modern editor must be to the hundred and one practical business matters which to-day enter into and form so large a part of the editorial duties. We may question whether women have as yet had sufficient experience in the world of business to cope successfully with the material questions of a pivotal editorial position. Then, again, it is absolutely essential in the conduct of a magazine with

108

a feminine or home appeal to have on the editorial staff women who are experts in their line; and the truth is that women will work infinitely better under the direction of a man than of a woman.

It would seem from the present outlook that, for some time, at least, the so-called woman's magazine of large purpose and wide vision is very likely to be edited by a man. It is a question, however, whether the day of the woman's magazine, as we have known it, is not passing. Already the day has gone for the woman's magazine built on the old lines which now seem so grotesque and feeble in the light of modern growth. The interests of women and of men are being brought closer with the years, and it will not be long before they will entirely merge. This means a constantly diminishing necessity for the distinctly feminine magazine.

Naturally, there will always be a field in the essentially feminine pursuits which have no place in the life of a man, but these are rapidly being cared for by books, gratuitously distributed, issued by the manufacturers of distinctly feminine and domestic wares; for such publications the best talent is being employed, and the results are placed within easy access of women, by means of newspaper advertisement, the store-counter, or the mails. These will sooner or later—and much sooner than later—supplant the practical portions of the woman's magazine, leaving only the general contents, which are equally interesting to men and to women. Hence the field for the magazine with the essentially feminine appeal is contracting rather than broadening, and it is likely to contract much more rapidly in the future.

The field was altogether different when Edward Bok entered it in 1889. It was not only wide open, but fairly

crying out to be filled. The day of *Godey's Lady's Book*
had passed; *Peterson's Magazine* was breathing its last;
and the home or women's magazines that had attempted
to take their place were sorry affairs. It was this consciousness of a void ready to be filled that made the Philadelphia experiment so attractive to the embryo editor. He
looked over the field and reasoned that if such magazines
as did exist could be fairly successful, if women were ready
to buy such, how much greater response would there be
to a magazine of higher standards, of larger initiative—
a magazine that would be an authoritative clearing-house
for all the problems confronting women in the home, that
brought itself closely into contact with those problems
and tried to solve them in an entertaining and efficient way;
and yet a magazine of uplift and inspiration: a magazine,
in other words, that would give light and leading in the
woman's world.

The method of editorial expression in the magazines
of 1889 was also distinctly vague and prohibitively imper-
sonal. The public knew the name of scarcely a single editor
of a magazine: there was no personality that stood out in
the mind: the accepted editorial expression was the in-
definite "we"; no one ventured to use the first person singular and talk intimately to the reader. Edward Bok's
biographical reading had taught him that the American
public loved a personality: that it was always ready to recognize and follow a leader, provided, of course, that the
qualities of leadership were demonstrated. He felt the time
had come—the reference here and elsewhere is always to
the realm of popular magazine literature appealing to a
very wide audience—for the editor of some magazine to
project his personality through the printed page and to
convince the public that he was not an oracle removed from

the people, but a real human being who could talk and not merely write on paper.

He saw, too, that the average popular magazine of 1889 failed of large success because it wrote down to the public —a grievous mistake that so many editors have made and still make. No one wants to be told, either directly or indirectly, that he knows less than he does, or even that he knows as little as he does: every one is benefited by the opposite implication, and the public will always follow the leader who comprehends this bit of psychology. There is always a happy medium between shooting over the public's head and shooting too far under it. And it is because of the latter aim that we find the modern popular magazine the worthless thing that, in so many instances, it is to-day.

It is the rare editor who rightly gauges his public psychology. Perhaps that is why, in the enormous growth of the modern magazine, there have been produced so few successful editors. The average editor is obsessed with the idea of "giving the public what it wants," whereas, in fact, the public, while it knows what it wants when it sees it, cannot clearly express its wants, and never wants the thing that it does ask for, although it thinks it does at the time. But woe to the editor and his periodical if he heeds that siren voice!

The editor has, therefore, no means of finding it out aforehand by putting his ear to the ground. Only by the simplest rules of psychology can he edit rightly so that he may lead, and to the average editor of to-day, it is to be feared, psychology is a closed book. His mind is all too often focussed on the circulation and advertising, and all too little on the intangibles that will bring to his periodical the results essential in these respects.

The editor is the pivot of a magazine. On him everything turns. If his gauge of the public is correct, readers will come: they cannot help coming to the man who has something to say himself, or who presents writers who have. And if the reader comes, the advertiser must come. He must go where his largest market is: where the buyers are. The advertiser, instead of being the most difficult factor in a magazine proposition, as is so often mistakenly thought, is, in reality, the simplest. He has no choice but to advertise in the successful periodical. He must come along. The editor need never worry about him. If the advertiser shuns the periodical's pages, the fault is rarely that of the advertiser: the editor can generally look for the reason nearer home.

One of Edward Bok's first acts as editor was to offer a series of prizes for the best answers to three questions he put to his readers: what in the magazine did they like least and why; what did they like best and why; and what omitted feature or department would they like to see installed? Thousands of answers came, and these the editor personally read carefully and classified. Then he gave his readers' suggestions back to them in articles and departments, but never on the level suggested by them. He gave them the subjects they asked for, but invariably on a slightly higher plane; and each year he raised the standard a notch. He always kept "a huckleberry or two" ahead of his readers. His psychology was simple: come down to the level which the public sets and it will leave you at the moment you do it. It always expects of its leaders that they shall keep a notch above or a step ahead. The American public always wants something a little better than it asks for, and the succesful man, in catering to it, is he who follows this golden rule.

CHAPTER XIII

BUILDING UP A MAGAZINE

Edward Bok has often been referred to as the one "who made *The Ladies' Home Journal* out of nothing," who "built it from the ground up," or, in similar terms, implying that when he became its editor in 1889 the magazine was practically non-existent. This is far from the fact. The magazine was begun in 1883, and had been edited by Mrs. Cyrus H. K. Curtis, for six years, under her maiden name of Louisa Knapp, before Bok undertook its editorship. Mrs. Curtis had laid a solid foundation of principle and policy for the magazine: it had achieved a circulation of 440,000 copies a month when she transferred the editorship, and it had already acquired such a standing in the periodical world as to attract the advertisements of Charles Scribner's Sons, which Mr. Doubleday, and later Bok himself, gave to the Philadelphia magazine—advertising which was never given lightly, or without the most careful investigation of the worth of the circulation of a periodical.

What every magazine publisher knows as the most troublous years in the establishment of a periodical, the first half-dozen years of its existence, had already been weathered by the editor and publisher. The wife as editor and the husband as publisher had combined to lay a solid basis upon which Bok had only to build: his task was simply to rear a structure upon the foundation already laid. It is to the vision and to the genius of the first editor of *The Ladies' Home Journal* that the unprecedented success

113

of the magazine is primarily due. It was the purpose and
the policy of making a magazine of authoritative service
for the womanhood of America, a service which would visu-
alize for womanhood its highest domestic estate, that had
won success for the periodical from its inception. It is difficult to believe, in the multiplicity of similar magazines to-
day, that such a purpose was new; that *The Ladies' Home
Journal* was a path-finder; but the convincing proof is
found in the fact that all the later magazines of this class
have followed in the wake of the periodical conceived by
Mrs. Curtis, and have ever since been its imitators.

When Edward Bok succeeded Mrs. Curtis, he immediately encountered another popular misconception of a
woman's magazine—the conviction that if a man is the editor of a periodical with a distinctly feminine appeal, he
must, as the term goes, "understand women." If Bok
had believed this to be true, he would never have assumed
the position. How deeply rooted is this belief was brought
home to him on every hand when his decision to accept
the Philadelphia position was announced. His mother,
knowing her son better than did any one else, looked at
him with amazement. She could not believe that he was
serious in his decision to cater to women's needs when he
knew so little about them. His friends, too, were intensely
amused, and took no pains to hide their amusement from
him. They knew him to be the very opposite of "a lady's
man," and when they were not convulsed with hilarity
they were incredulous and marvelled.

No man, perhaps, could have been chosen for the position who had a less intimate knowledge of women. Bok
had no sister, no women confidantes: he had lived with
and for his mother. She was the only woman he really
knew or who really knew him. His boyhood days had been

too full of poverty and struggle to permit him to mingle with the opposite sex. And it is a curious fact that Edward Bok's instinctive attitude toward women was that of avoidance. He did not dislike women, but it could not be said that he liked them. They had never interested him. Of women, therefore, he knew little; of their needs less. Nor had he the slightest desire, even as an editor, to know them better or to seek to understand them. Even at that age, he knew that, as a man, he could not, no matter what effort he might make, and he let it go at that.

What he saw in the position was not the need to know women; he could employ women for that purpose. He perceived clearly that the editor of a magazine was largely an executive: his was principally the work of direction; of studying currents and movements, watching their formation, their tendency, their efficacy if advocated or translated into actuality, and then selecting from the horizon those that were for the best interests of the home. For a home was something which Edward Bok did understand. He had always lived in one; had struggled to keep it together, and he knew every inch of the hard road that makes for domestic permanence amid adverse financial conditions. And at the home he aimed rather than at the woman in it.

And with his own limited knowledge of the sex, he needed, and none knew it better than did he, the ablest women he could obtain to help him realize his ideals. Their personal opinions of him did not matter so long as he could command their best work. Sooner or later, when his purposes were better understood, they might alter those opinions. For that he could afford to wait. But he could not wait to get their work.

By this time the editor had come to see that the power

of a magazine might lie more securely behind the printed page than in it. He had begun to accustom his readers to writing to his editors upon all conceivable problems.

This he decided to encourage. He employed an expert in each line of feminine endeavor, upon the distinct understanding that the most scrupulous attention should be given to her correspondence: that every letter, no matter how inconsequential, should be answered quickly, fully, and courteously, with the questioner always encouraged to come again if any problem of whatever nature came to her. He told his editors that ignorance on any question was a misfortune, not a crime; and he wished their correspondence treated in the most courteous and helpful spirit.

Step by step, the editor built up this service behind the magazine until he had a staff of thirty-five editors on the monthly pay-roll; in each issue, he proclaimed the willingness of these editors to answer immediately any questions by mail, he encouraged and cajoled his readers to form the habit of looking upon his magazine as a great clearinghouse of information. Before long, the letters streamed in by the tens of thousands during a year. The editor still encouraged, and the total ran into the hundreds of thousands, until during the last year, before the service was finally stopped by the Great War in 1917, the yearly correspondence totalled nearly a million letters.

The lack of opportunity for an education in Bok's own life led him to cast about for some plan whereby an education might be obtained without expense by any one who desired. He finally hit upon the simple plan of substituting free scholarships for the premiums then so frequently offered by periodicals for subscriptions secured. Free musical education at the leading conservatories was first offered to any girl who would secure a certain number of subscrip-

THE GRANDMOTHER

Who counselled each of her children to make the world a better and more beautiful place
to live in—a counsel which is now being carried on by her grandchildren,
one of whom is Edward Bok

tions to *The Ladies' Home Journal*, the complete offer being a year's free tuition, with free room, free board, free piano in her own room, and all travelling expenses paid. The plan was an immediate success: the solicitation of a subscription by a girl desirous of educating herself made an irresistible appeal.

This plan was soon extended, so as to include all the girls' colleges, and finally all the men's colleges, so that a free education might be possible at any educational institution. So comprehensive it became that to the close of 1919, one thousand four hundred and fifty-five free scholarships had been awarded. The plan has now been in operation long enough to have produced some of the leading singers and instrumental artists of the day, whose names are familiar to all, as well as instructors in colleges and scores of teachers; and to have sent several score of men into conspicuous positions in the business and professional world.

Edward Bok has always felt that but for his own inability to secure an education, and his consequent desire for self-improvement, the realization of the need in others might not have been so strongly felt by him, and that his plan whereby thousands of others were benefited might never have been realized.

It was this comprehensive personal service, built up back of the magazine from the start, that gave the periodical so firm and unique a hold on its clientele. It was not the printed word that was its chief power: scores of editors who have tried to study and diagnose the appeal of the magazine from the printed page, have remained baffled at the remarkable confidence elicited from its readers. They never looked back of the magazine, and therefore failed to discover its secret. Bok went through three financial panics with the magazine, and while other periodicals severely suffered from diminished circulation at such times, *The Ladies' Home Journal* always held its own. Thousands of women had been directly helped by the magazine; it had not remained an inanimate printed thing, but had become a vital need in the personal lives of its readers.

So intimate had become this relation, so efficient was the service rendered, that its readers could not be pried loose from it; where women were willing and ready, when the domestic pinch came, to let go of other reading matter, they explained to their husbands or fathers that *The Ladies' Home Journal* was a necessity—they did not feel that they could do without it. The very quality for which the magazine had been held up to ridicule by the unknowing and unthinking had become, with hundreds of thousands of women, its source of power and the bulwark of its success.

Bok was beginning to realize the vision which had lured him from New York: that of putting into the field of American magazines a periodical that should become such a clearing-house as virtually to make it an institution.

He felt that, for the present at least, he had sufficiently established the personal contact with his readers through the more intimate departments, and decided to devote his efforts to the literary features of the magazine.

The newspaper paragraphers were now having a delightful time with Edward Bok and his woman's magazine, and he was having a delightful time with them. The editor's publicity sense made him realize how valuable for his purposes was all this free advertising. The paragraphers believed, in their hearts, that they were annoying the young editor; they tried to draw his fire through their articles. But he kept quiet, put his tongue in his cheek.

and determined to give them some choice morsels for their wit.

He conceived the idea of making familiar to the public the women who were back of the successful men of the day. He felt sure that his readers wanted to know about these women. But to attract his newspaper friends he labelled the series, "Unknown Wives of Well-Known Men" and "Clever Daughters of Clever Men."

The alliterative titles at once attracted the paragraphers; they fell upon them like hungry trout, and a perfect fusillade of paragraphs began. This is exactly what the editor wanted; and he followed these two series immediately by inducing the daughter of Charles Dickens to write of "My Father as I Knew Him," and Mrs. Henry Ward Beecher, of "Mr. Beecher as I Knew Him." Bok now felt that he had given the newspapers enough ammunition to last for some time; and he turned his attention to building up a more permanent basis for his magazine.

The two authors of that day who commanded more attention than any others were William Dean Howells and Rudyard Kipling. Bok knew that these two would give to his magazine the literary quality that it needed, and so he laid them both under contribution. He bought Mr. Howells's new novel, "The Coast of Bohemia," and arranged that Kipling's new novelette upon which he was working should come to the magazine. Neither the public nor the magazine editors had expected Bok to break out along these more permanent lines, and magazine publishers began to realize that a new competitor had sprung up in Philadelphia. Bok knew they would feel this; so before he announced Mr. Howells's new novel, he contracted with the novelist to follow this with his autobiography. This surprised the editors of the older magazines, for they realized that the Philadelphia editor had completely tied up the leading novelist of the day for his next two years' output.

Meanwhile, in order that the newspapers might be well supplied with barbs for their shafts, he published an entire number of his magazine written by the daughters of famous men. This unique issue presented contributions by the daughters of Charles Dickens, Nathaniel Hawthorne, President Harrison, Horace Greeley, William M. Thackeray, William Dean Howells, General Sherman, Jefferson Davis, Mr. Gladstone, and a score of others. This issue simply filled the paragraphers with glee. Then once more Bok turned to articles calculated to cement the foundation for a more permanent structure.

The material that the editor was publishing and the authors that he was laying under contribution began to have marked effect upon the circulation of the magazine, and it was not long before the original figures were doubled, an edition—enormous for that day—of seven hundred and fifty thousand copies was printed and sold each month, the magical figure of a million was in sight, and the periodical was rapidly taking its place as one of the largest successes of the day.

Mr. Curtis's single proprietorship of the magazine had been changed into a corporation called The Curtis Publishing Company, with a capital of five hundred thousand dollars, with Mr. Curtis as president, and Bok as vice-president.

The magazine had by no means an easy road to travel financially. The doubling of the subscription price to one dollar per year had materially checked the income for the time being; the huge advertising bills, sometimes exceeding three hundred thousand dollars a year, were difficult to pay;

large credit had to be obtained, and the banks were carrying a considerable quantity of Mr. Curtis's notes. But Mr. Curtis never wavered in his faith in his proposition and his editor. In the first he invested all he had and could borrow, and to the latter he gave his undivided support. The two men worked together rather as father and son—as, curiously enough, they were to be later—than as employer and employee. To Bok, the daily experience of seeing Mr. Curtis finance his proposition in sums that made the publishing world of that day gasp with sceptical astonishment was a wonderful opportunity, of which the editor took full advantage so as to learn the intricacies of a world which up to that time he had known only in a limited way.

What attracted Bok immensely to Mr. Curtis's methods was their perfect simplicity and directness. He believed absolutely in the final outcome of his proposition: where others saw mist and failure ahead, he saw clear weather and the port of success. Never did he waver: never did he deflect from his course. He knew no path save the direct one that led straight to success, and, through his eyes, he made Bok see it with equal clarity until Bok wondered why others could not see it. But they could not. Cyrus Curtis would never be able, they said, to come out from under the load he had piled up. Where they differed from Mr. Curtis was in their lack of vision: they could not see what he saw!

It has been said that Mr. Curtis banished patent-medicine advertisements from his magazine only when he could afford to do so. That is not true, as a simple incident will show. In the early days, he and Bok were opening the mail one Friday full of anxiety because the pay-roll was due that evening, and there was not enough money in the bank to meet it. From one of the letters dropped a certified check for five figures for a contract equal to five pages in the magazine. It was a welcome sight, for it meant an easy meeting of the pay-roll for that week and two succeeding weeks. But the check was from a manufacturing patent-medicine company. Without a moment's hesitation, Mr. Curtis slipped it back into the envelope, saying: "Of course, *that* we can't take." He returned the check, never gave the matter a second thought, and went out and borrowed more money to meet his pay-roll.

With all respect to American publishers, there are very few who could have done this—or indeed, would do it to-day, under similar conditions—particularly in that day when it was the custom for all magazines to accept patent-medicine advertising; *The Ladies' Home Journal* was practically the only publication of standing in the United States refusing that class of business!

Bok now saw advertising done on a large scale by a man who believed in plenty of white space surrounding the announcement in the advertisement. He paid Mr. Howells $10,000 for his autobiography, and Mr. Curtis spent $50,000 in advertising it. "It is not expense," he would explain to Bok, "it is investment. We are investing in a trademark. It will all come back in time." And when the first $100,000 did not come back as Mr. Curtis figured, he would send another $100,000 after it, and then both came back.

Bok's experience in advertisement writing was now to stand him in excellent stead. He wrote all the advertisements, and from that day to the day of his retirement, practically every advertisement of the magazine was written by him.

Mr. Curtis believed that the editor should write the advertisements of a magazine's articles. "You are the one

who knows them, what is in them and your purpose," he
said to Bok, who keenly enjoyed this advertisement writing. He put less and less in his advertisements. Mr.
Curtis made them larger and larger in the space which they
occupied in the media used. In this way *The Ladies' Home
Journal* advertisements became distinctive for their use of
white space, and as the advertising world began to say:
"You can't miss them." Only one feature was advertised
at one time, but the "feature" was always carefully selected for its wide popular appeal, and then Mr. Curtis
spared no expense to advertise it abundantly. As much
as $400,000 was spent in one year in advertising only a
few features—a gigantic sum in those days, approached
by no other periodical. But Mr. Curtis believed in showing
the advertising world that he was willing to take his own
medicine.

Naturally, such a campaign of publicity announcing
the most popular attractions offered by any magazine of
the day had but one effect: the circulation leaped forward
by bounds, and the advertising columns of the magazine
rapidly filled up.

The success of *The Ladies' Home Journal* began to look
like an assured fact, even to the most sceptical.

As a matter of fact, it was only at its beginning, as
both publisher and editor knew. But they desired to fill
the particular field of the magazine so quickly and fully
that there would be small room for competition. The
woman's magazine field was to belong to them!

CHAPTER XIV

MEETING A REVERSE OR TWO

With the hitherto unreached magazine circulation of a million copies a month in sight, Edward Bok decided to give a broader scope to the periodical. He was determined to lay under contribution not only the most famous writers of the day, but also to seek out those well-known persons who usually did not contribute to the magazines; always keeping in mind the popular appeal of his material, but likewise aiming constantly to widen its scope and gradually to lift its standard.

The editor was very desirous of securing something for his magazine that would delight children, and he hit upon the idea of trying to induce Lewis Carroll to write another *Alice in Wonderland* series. He was told by English friends that this would be difficult, since the author led a secluded life at Oxford and hardly ever admitted any one into his confidence. But Bok wanted to beard the lion in his den, and an Oxford graduate volunteered to introduce him to an Oxford don through whom, if it were at all possible, he could reach the author. The journey to Oxford was made, and Bok was introduced to the don, who turned out to be no less a person than the original possessor of the highly colored vocabulary of the "White Rabbit" of the *Alice* stories.

"Impossible," immediately declared the don. "You couldn't persuade Dodgson to consider it." Bok, however, persisted, and it so happened that the don liked what he called "American perseverance."

"Well, come along," he said. "We'll beard the lion in his den, as you say, and see what happens. You know, of course, that it is the Reverend Charles L. Dodgson that we are going to see, and I must introduce you to that person, not to Lewis Carroll. He is a tutor in mathematics here, as you doubtless know; lives a rigidly secluded life; dislikes strangers; makes no friends; and yet withal is one of the most delightful men in the world if he wants to be."

But as it happened upon this special occasion when Bok was introduced to him in his chambers in Tom Quad, Mr. Dodgson did not "want to be" delightful. There was no doubt that back of the studied reserve was a kindly, charming, gracious gentleman, but Bok's profession had been mentioned and the author was on rigid guard.

When Bok explained that one of the special reasons for his journey from America was to see him, the Oxford mathematician sufficiently softened to ask the editor to sit down. Bok then broached his mission.

"You are quite in error, Mr. Bok," was the Dodgson comment. "You are not speaking to the person you think you are addressing."

For a moment Bok was taken aback. Then he decided to go right to the point.

"Do I understand, Mr. Dodgson, that you are not 'Lewis Carroll'; that you did not write *Alice in Wonderland?*"

For an answer the tutor rose, went into another room, and returned with a book which he handed to Bok. "This is my book," he said simply. It was entitled *An Elementary Treatise on Determinants*, by C. L. Dodgson. When he looked up, Bok found the author's eyes riveted on him.

"Yes," said Bok. "I know, Mr. Dodgson. If I remember correctly, this is the same book of which you sent a copy to Her Majesty, Queen Victoria, when she wrote to you for a personal copy of your *Alice*."

Dodgson made no comment. The face was absolutely without expression save a kindly compassion intended to convey to the editor that he was making a terrible mistake.

"As I said to you in the beginning, Mr. Bok, you are in error. You are not speaking to 'Lewis Carroll.'" And then: "Is this the first time you have visited Oxford?"

Bok said it was; and there followed the most delightful two hours with the Oxford mathematician and the Oxford don, walking about and into the wonderful college buildings, and afterward the three had a bite of lunch together. But all efforts to return to "Lewis Carroll" were futile. While saying good-by to his host, Bok remarked:

"I can't help expressing my disappointment, Mr. Dodgson, in my quest in behalf of the thousands of American children who love you and who would so gladly welcome 'Lewis Carroll' back."

The mention of children and their love for him momentarily had its effect. For an instant a different light came into the eyes, and Bok instinctively realized Dodgson was about to say something. But he checked himself. Bok had almost caught him off his guard.

"I am sorry," he finally said at the parting at the door, "that you should be disappointed, for the sake of the children as well as for your own sake. I only regret that I cannot remove the disappointment."

As they later walked to the station, the don said: "That is his attitude toward all, even toward me. He is not 'Lewis Carroll' to any one; is extremely sensitive on the point, and will not acknowledge his identity. That is why he lives so much to himself. He is in daily dread that some one will mention *Alice* in his presence. Curious, but there it is."

Edward Bok's next quest was to be even more disappointing; he was never even to reach the presence of the person he sought. This was Florence Nightingale, the Crimean nurse. Bok was desirous of securing her own story of her experiences, but on every hand he found an unwillingness even to take him to her house. "No use," said everybody. "She won't see any one. Hates publicity and all that sort of thing, and shuns the public." Nevertheless, the editor journeyed to the famous nurse's home on South Street, in the West End of London, only to be told that "Miss Nightingale never receives strangers."

"But I am not a stranger," insisted the editor. "I am one of her friends from America. Please take my card to her."

This mollified the faithful secretary, but the word instantly came back that Miss Nightingale was not receiving any one that day. Bok wrote her a letter asking for an appointment, which was never answered. Then he wrote another, took it personally to the house, and awaited an answer, only to receive the message that "Miss Nightingale says there is no answer to the letter."

Bok had with such remarkable uniformity secured whatever he sought, that these experiences were new to him. Frankly, they puzzled him. He was not easily baffled, but baffled he now was, and that twice in succession. Turn as he might, he could find no way in which to reopen an approach to either the Oxford tutor or the Crimean nurse. They were plainly too much for him, and he had to acknowledge his defeat. The experience was good for him; he did not realize this at the time, nor did he enjoy the sensation of not getting what he wanted. Nevertheless, a reverse or two was due. Not that his success was having any undesirable effect upon him; his Dutch common sense saved him from any such calamity. But at thirty years of age it is not good for any one, no matter how well balanced, to have things come his way too fast and too consistently. And here were breaks. He could not have everything he wanted, and it was just as well that he should find that out.

In his next quest he found himself again opposed by his London friends. Unable to secure a new *Alice in Wonderland* for his child readers, he determined to give them Kate Greenaway. But here he had selected another recluse. Everybody discouraged him. The artist never saw visitors, he was told, and she particularly shunned editors and publishers. Her own publishers confessed that Miss Greenaway was inaccessible to them. "We conduct all our business with her by correspondence. I have never seen her personally myself," said a member of the firm.

Bok inwardly decided that two failures in two days were sufficient, and he made up his mind that there should not be a third. He took a bus for the long ride to Hampstead Heath, where the illustrator lived, and finally stood before a picturesque Queen Anne house that one would have recognized at once, with its lower story of red brick, its upper part covered with red tiles, its windows of every size and shape, as the inspiration of Kate Greenaway's pictures. As it turned out later, Miss Greenaway's sister opened the door and told the visitor that Miss Greenaway was not at home.

"But, pardon me, has not Miss Greenaway returned? Is not that she?" asked Bok, as he indicated a figure just coming down the stairs. And as the sister turned to see, Bok stepped into the hall. At least he was inside! Bok had never seen a photograph of Miss Greenaway, he did not know that the figure coming down-stairs was the artist; but his instinct had led him right, and good fortune was with him.

He now introduced himself to Kate Greenaway, and explained that one of his objects in coming to London was to see her on behalf of thousands of American children. Naturally there was nothing for the illustrator to do but to welcome her visitor. She took him into the garden, where he saw at once that he was seated under the apple-tree of Miss Greenaway's pictures. It was in full bloom, a veritable picture of spring loveliness. Bok's love for nature pleased the artist and when he recognized the cat. that sauntered up, he could see that he was making head-way. But when he explained his profession and stated his errand, the atmosphere instantly changed. Miss Green-away conveyed the unmistakable impression that she had been trapped, and Bok realized at once that he had a long and difficult road ahead.

Still, negotiate it he must and he did! And after lunch-eon in the garden, with the cat in his lap, Miss Greenaway perceptibly thawed out, and when the editor left late that afternoon he had the promise of the artist that she would do her first magazine work for him. That promise was kept monthly, and for nearly two years her articles ap-peared, with satisfaction to Miss Greenaway and with great success to the magazine.

Bok now devoted his attention to strengthening the fiction in his magazine. He sought Mark Twain, and bought his two new stories; he secured from Bret Harte a tale which he had just finished, and then ran the gamut of the best fiction writers of the day, and secured their best output. Marion Crawford, Conan Doyle, Sarah Orne Jewett, John Kendrick Bangs, Kate Douglas Wiggin, Hamlin Garland, Mrs. Burton Harrison, Elizabeth Stuart Phelps, Mary E. Wilkins, Jerome K. Jerome, Anthony Hope, Joel Chandler Harris, and others followed in rapid succession.

He next turned for a moment to his religious department, decided that it needed a freshening of interest, and secured Dwight L. Moody, whose evangelical work was then so prominently in the public eye, to conduct "Mr. Moody's Bible Class" in the magazine—practically a study of the stated Bible lesson of the month with explanation in Moody's simple and effective style.

The authors for whom the *Journal* was now publishing attracted the attention of all the writers of the day, and the supply of good material became too great for its capacity. Bok studied the mechanical make-up, and felt that by some method he must find more room in the front portion. He had allotted the first third of the magazine to the general literary contents and the latter two-thirds to departmental features. Toward the close of the number, the departments narrowed down from full pages to single columns with advertisements on each side.

One day Bok was handling a story by Rudyard Kipling which had overrun the space allowed for it in the front. The story had come late, and the rest of the front portion of the magazine had gone to press. The editor was in a quandary what to do with the two remaining columns of the Kipling tale. There were only two pages open, and these were at the back. He remade those pages, and continued the story from pages 6 and 7 to pages 38 and 39.

At once Bok saw that this was an instance where "necessity was the mother of invention." He realized that if he could run some of his front material over to the back he would relieve the pressure at the front, present a more varied contents there, and make his advertisements more valuable by putting them next to the most expensive material in the magazine.

In the next issue he combined some of his smaller departments in the back; and thus, in 1896, he inaugurated the method of "running over into the back" which has now become a recognized principle in the make-up of magazines of larger size. At first, Bok's readers objected, but he explained why he did it; that they were the benefiters by the plan; and, so far as readers can be satisfied with what is, at best, an awkward method of presentation, they were content. To-day the practice is undoubtedly followed to excess, some magazines carrying as much as eighty and ninety columns over from the front to the back; from such abuse it will, of course, free itself either by a return to the original method of make-up or by the adoption of some other less irritating plan.

In his reading about the America of the past, Bok had been impressed by the unusual amount of interesting personal material that constituted what is termed unwritten history—original events of tremendous personal appeal in which great personalities figured but which had not sufficient historical importance to have been included in American history. Bok determined to please his older readers by harking back to the past and at the same time acquainting the younger generation with the picturesque events which had preceded their time.

He also believed that if he could "dress up" the past, he could arrest the attention of a generation which was too likely to boast of its interest only in the present and the

future. He took a course of reading and consulted with
Mr. Charles A. Dana, editor of the *New York Sun*, who
had become interested in his work and had written him
several voluntary letters of commendation. Mr. Dana gave
material help in the selection of subjects and writers; and
was intensely amused and interested by the manner in
which his youthful confrère "dressed up" the titles of what
might otherwise have looked like commonplace articles.

"I know," said Bok to the elder editor, "it smacks
a little of the sensational, Mr. Dana, but the purpose I
have in mind of showing the young people of to-day that
some great things happened before they came on the stage
seems to me to make it worth while."

Mr. Dana agreed with this view, supplemented every
effort of the Philadelphia editor in several subsequent
talks, and in 1897 *The Ladies' Home Journal* began one of
the most popular series it ever published. It was called
"Great Personal Events," and the picturesque titles explained them. He first pictured the enthusiastic evening
"When Jenny Lind Sang in Castle Garden," and, as Bok
added to pique curiosity, "when people paid $20 to sit in
rowboats to hear the Swedish nightingale."

This was followed by an account of the astonishing
episode "When Henry Ward Beecher Sold Slaves in Plymouth Pulpit"; the picturesque journey "When Louis
Kossuth Rode Up Broadway"; the triumphant tour "When
General Grant Went Round the World"; the forgotten
story of "When an Actress Was the Lady of the White
House"; the sensational striking of the rich silver vein
"When Mackay Struck the Great Bonanza"; the hitherto
little-known instance "When Louis Philippe Taught School
in Philadelphia"; and even the lesser-known fact of the
residence of the brother of Napoleon Bonaparte in America,

"When the King of Spain Lived on the Banks of the Schuyl-kill"; while the story of "When John Wesley Preached in Georgia" surprised nearly every Methodist, as so few had known that the founder of their church had ever visited America. Each month picturesque event followed graphic happening, and never was unwritten history more readily read by the young, or the memories of the older folk more catered to than in this series which won new friends for the magazine on every hand.

CHAPTER XV

The influence of his grandfather and the injunction of his grandmother to her sons that each "should make the world a better or a more beautiful place to live in" now began to be manifest in the grandson. Edward Bok was unconscious that it was this influence. What directly led him to the signal piece of construction in which he engaged was the wretched architecture of small houses. As he travelled through the United States he was appalled by it. Where the houses were not positively ugly, they were, to him, repellently ornate. Money was wasted on useless turrets, filigree work, or machine-made ornamentation. Bok found out that these small householders never employed an architect, but that the houses were put up by builders from their own plans.

Bok turned to *The Ladies' Home Journal* as his medium for making the small-house architecture of America better. He realized the limitation of space, but decided to do the best he could under the circumstances. He believed he might serve thousands of his readers if he could make it possible for them to secure, at moderate cost, plans for well-designed houses by the leading domestic architects in the country. He consulted a number of architects, only to find them unalterably opposed to the idea. They disliked the publicity of magazine presentation; prices differed too much in various parts of the country; and they did not care to risk the criticism of their contemporaries. It was "cheapening" their profession!

Bok saw that he should have to blaze the way and demonstrate the futility of these arguments. At last he persuaded one architect to co-operate with him, and in 1895 began the publication of a series of houses which could be built, approximately, for from one thousand five hundred dollars to five thousand dollars. The idea attracted attention at once, and the architect-author was swamped with letters and inquiries regarding his plans.

This proved Bok's instinct to be correct as to the public willingness to accept such designs; upon this proof he succeeded in winning over two additional architects to make plans. He offered his readers full building specifications and plans to scale of the houses with estimates from four builders in different parts of the United States for five dollars a set. The plans and specifications were so complete in every detail that any builder could build the house from them.

A storm of criticism now arose from architects and builders all over the country, the architects claiming that Bok was taking "the bread out of their mouths" by the sale of plans, and local builders vigorously questioned the accuracy of the estimates. But Bok knew he was right and persevered.

Slowly but surely he won the approval of the leading architects, who saw that he was appealing to a class of house-builders who could not afford to pay an architect's fee, and that, with his wide circulation, he might become an influence for better architecture through these small houses. The sets of plans and specifications sold by the thousands. It was not long before the magazine was able to present small-house plans by the foremost architects of the country, whose services the average householder could otherwise never have dreamed of securing.

Bok not only saw an opportunity to better the exterior of the small houses, but he determined that each plan published should provide for two essentials: every servant's room should have two windows to insure cross-ventilation, and contain twice the number of cubic feet usually given to such rooms; and in place of the American parlor, which he considered a useless room, should be substituted either a living-room or a library. He did not point to these improvements; every plan simply presented the larger servant's room and did not present a parlor. It is a singular fact that of the tens of thousands of plans sold, not a purchaser ever noticed the absence of a parlor except one woman in Brookline, Mass., who, in erecting a group of twenty-five "*Journal* houses," discovered after she had built ten that not one contained a parlor!

For nearly twenty-five years Bok continued to publish pictures of houses and plans. Entire colonies of "*Ladies' Home Journal* houses" have sprung up, and building promoters have built complete suburban developments with them. How many of these homes have been erected it is, of course, impossible to say; the number certainly runs into the thousands.

It was one of the most constructive and far-reaching pieces of work that Bok did during his editorial career—a fact now recognized by all architects. Shortly before Stanford White passed away, he wrote: "I firmly believe that Edward Bok has more completely influenced American domestic architecture for the better than any man in this generation. When he began, I was short-sighted enough to discourage him, and refused to co-operate with him. If Bok came to me now, I would not only make plans for him, but I would waive any fee for them in retribution for my early mistake."

Bok then turned to the subject of the garden for the small house, and the development of the grounds around the homes which he had been instrumental in putting on the earth. He encountered no opposition here. The publication of small gardens for small houses finally ran into hundreds of pages, the magazine supplying planting plans and full directions as to when and how to plant—this time without cost.

Next the editor decided to see what he could do for the better and simpler furnishing of the small American home. Here was a field almost limitless in possible improvement, but he wanted to approach it in a new way. The best method baffled him until one day he met a woman friend who told him that she was on her way to a funeral at a friend's home.

"I didn't know you were so well acquainted with Mrs. S——," said Bok.

"I wasn't, as a matter of fact," replied the woman. "I'll be perfectly frank; I am going to the funeral just to see how Mrs. S——'s house is furnished. She was always thought to have great taste, you know, and, whether you know it or not, a woman is always keen to look into another woman's home."

Bok realized that he had found the method of presentation for his interior-furnishing plan if he could secure photographs of the most carefully furnished homes in America. He immediately employed the best available expert, and within six months there came to him an assorted collection of over a thousand photographs of well-furnished rooms. The best were selected, and a series of photographic pages called "Inside of 100 Homes" was begun. The editor's woman friend had correctly pointed the way to him, for this series won for his magazine the enviable distinction of being the first magazine of standing to reach the then marvellous record of a circulation of one million copies a month. The editions containing the series were sold out as fast as they could be printed.

The editor followed this up with another successful series, again pictorial. He realized that to explain good taste in furnishing by text was almost impossible. So he started a series of all-picture pages called "Good Taste and Bad Taste." He presented a chair that was bad in lines and either useless or uncomfortable to sit in, and explained where and why it was bad; and then put a good chair next to it, and explained where and why it was good.

The lesson to the eye was simply and directly effective; the pictures told their story as no printed word could have done, and furniture manufacturers and dealers all over the country, feeling the pressure from their customers, began to put on the market the tables, chairs, divans, bedsteads, and dressing-tables which the magazine was portraying as examples of good taste. It was amazing that, within five years, the physical appearance of domestic furniture in the stores completely changed.

The next undertaking was a systematic plan for improving the pictures on the walls of the American home. Bok was employing the best artists of the day: Edwin A. Abbey, Howard Pyle, Charles Dana Gibson, W. L. Taylor, Albert Lynch, Will H. Low, W. T. Smedley, Irving R. Wiles, and others. As his magazine was rolled to go through the mails, the pictures naturally suffered; Bok therefore decided to print a special edition of each important picture that he published, an edition on plate-paper, without text, and offered to his readers at ten cents a copy. Within a year he had sold nearly one hundred thousand copies, such pictures as W. L. Taylor's "The Hanging of the Crane" and "Home-Keeping Hearts" being particularly popular.

But all this was simply to lead up to the realization of Bok's cherished dream: the reproduction, in enormous numbers, of the greatest pictures in the world in their original colors. The plan, however, was not for the moment feasible: the cost of the four-color process was at that time prohibitive, and Bok had to abandon it. But he never lost sight of it. He knew the hour would come when he could carry it out, and he bided his time.

It was not until years later that his opportunity came, when he immediately made up his mind to seize it. The magazine had installed a battery of four-color presses; the color-work in the periodical was attracting universal attention, and after all stages of experimentation had been passed, Bok decided to make his dream a reality. He sought the co-operation of the owners of the greatest private art galleries in the country: J. Pierpont Morgan, Henry C. Frick, Joseph E. Widener, George W. Elkins, John G. Johnson, Charles P. Taft, Mrs. John L. Gardner, Charles L. Freer, Mrs. Havemeyer, and the owners of the Benjamin Altman Collection, and sought permission to reproduce their greatest paintings.

Although each felt doubtful of the ability of any process adequately to reproduce their masterpieces, the owners heartily co-operated with Bok. But Bok's co-editors discouraged his plan, since it would involve endless labor, the exclusive services of a corps of photographers and engravers, and the employment of the most careful pressmen available in the United States. The editor realized that the obstacles were numerous and that the expense would be enormous; but he felt sure that the American public was ready for his idea. And early in 1912 he announced his series and began its publication.

The most wonderful Rembrandt, Velasquez, Turner, Hobbema, Van Dyck, Raphael, Frans Hals, Romney, Gainsborough, Whistler, Corot, Mauve, Vermeer, Fragonard, Botticelli, and Titian reproductions followed in such rapid succession as fairly to daze the magazine readers. Four pictures were given in each number, and the faithfulness of the reproductions astonished even their owners. The success of the series was beyond Bok's own best hopes. He was printing and selling one and three-quarter million copies of each issue of his magazine; and before he was through he had presented to American homes throughout the breadth of the country over seventy million reproductions of forty separate masterpieces of art.

The dream of years had come true.

Bok had begun with the exterior of the small American house and made an impression upon it; he had brought the love of flowers into the hearts of thousands of small householders who had never thought they could have an artistic garden within a small area; he had changed the lines of furniture, and he had put better art on the walls of these homes. He had conceived a full-rounded scheme, and he had carried it out.

It was a peculiar satisfaction to Bok that Theodore Roosevelt once summed up this piece of work in these words: "Bok is the only man I ever heard of who changed, for the better, the architecture of an entire nation, and he did it so quickly and yet so effectively that we didn't know it was begun before it was finished. That is a mighty big job for one man to have done."

In 1905 and in previous years the casualties resulting from fireworks on the Fourth of July averaged from five to six thousand each year. The humorous weekly *Life* and the *Chicago Tribune* had been for some time agitating a restricted use of fireworks on the national fête day, but nevertheless the list of casualties kept creeping to higher figures. Bok decided to help by arousing the parents of America, in whose hands, after all, lay the remedy. He began a series of articles in the magazine, showing what had happened over a period of years, the criminality of allowing so many young lives to be snuffed out, and suggested how parents could help by prohibiting the deadly firecrackers and cannon, and how organizations could assist by influencing the passing of city ordinances. Each recurring January, *The Journal* returned to the subject, looking forward to the coming Fourth. It was a deep-rooted custom to eradicate, and powerful influences, in the form of thousands of small storekeepers, were at work upon local officials to pay no heed to the agitation. Gradually public opinion changed. The newspapers joined in the cry; women's organizations insisted upon action from local municipal bodies.

Finally, the civic spirit in Cleveland, Ohio, forced the passage of a city ordinance prohibiting the sale or use of fireworks on the Fourth. The following year when Cleveland reported no casualties as compared to an ugly list for the previous Fourth, a distinct impression was made upon other cities. Gradually, other municipalities took action, and year by year the list of Fourth of July casualties grew perceptibly shorter. New York City was now induced to join the list of prohibitive cities, by a personal appeal made to its mayor by Bok, and on the succeeding Fourth of July the city authorities, on behalf of the people of New York City, conferred a gold medal upon Edward Bok for his services in connection with the birth of the new Fourth in that city.

There still remains much to be done in cities as yet unawakened; but a comparison of the list of casualties of 1920 with that of 1905 proves the growth in enlightened public sentiment in fifteen years to have been steadily increasing. It is an instance not of Bok taking the initiative—that had already been taken—but of throwing the whole force of the magazine with those working in the field to help. It is the American woman who is primarily responsible for the safe and sane Fourth, so far as it already exists in this country to-day, and it is the American woman who can make it universal.

Bok's interest and knowledge in civic matters had now peculiarly prepared him for a personal adventure into community work. Merion, where he lived, was one of the most beautiful of the many suburbs that surround the Quaker City; but, like hundreds of similar communities, there had been developed in it no civic interest. Some of the most successful business men of Philadelphia lived in Merion; they had beautiful estates, which they maintained without regard to expense, but also without regard to the community as a whole. They were busy men; they came home tired after a day in the city; they considered themselves good citizens if they kept their own places sightly, but the idea of devoting their evenings to the problems of their community had never occurred to them before the evening when two of Bok's neighbors called to ask his help in forming a civic association.

A canvass of the sentiment of the neighborhood revealed the unanimous opinion that the experiment, if attempted, would be a failure,—an attitude not by any means confined to the residents of Merion! Bok decided to test it out; he called together twenty of his neighbors, put the suggestion before them and asked for two thousand dollars as a start, so that a paid secretary might be engaged, since the men themselves were too busy to attend to the details of the work. The amount was immediately subscribed, and in 1913 The Merion Civic Association applied for a charter and began its existence.

The leading men in the community were elected as a Board of Directors, and a salaried secretary was engaged to carry out the directions of the Board. The association adopted the motto: "To be nation right, and state right, we must first be community right." Three objectives were selected with which to attract community interest and membership: safety to life, in the form of proper police protection; safety to property, in the form of adequate hydrant and fire-engine service; and safety to health, in careful supervision of the water and milk used in the community.

"The three S's," as they were called, brought an immediate response. They were practical in their appeal, and members began to come in. The police force was increased from one officer at night and none in the day, to three at night and two during the day, and to this the Association added two special night officers of its own. Private detectives were intermittently brought in to "check up" and see that the service was vigilant. A fire hydrant was placed within seven hundred feet of every house, with the insurance rates reduced from twelve and one-half to thirty per cent; the services of three fire-engine companies was arranged for. Fire-gongs were introduced into the community to guard against danger from interruption of telephone service. The water supply was chemically analyzed each month and the milk supply carefully scrutinized. One hundred and fifty new electric-light posts specially designed, and pronounced by experts as the most beautiful and practical road lamps ever introduced into any community, were erected, making Merion the best-lighted community in its vicinity.

At every corner was erected an artistically designed cast-iron road sign; instead of the unsightly wooden ones, cast-iron automobile warnings were placed at every danger-ous spot; community bulletin-boards, to supplant the dis-play of notices on trees and poles, were placed at the rail-road station; litter-cans were distributed over the entire community; a new railroad station and post-office were secured; the station grounds were laid out as a garden by a landscape architect; new roads of permanent construction, from curb to curb, were laid down; uniform tree-planting along the roads was introduced; bird-houses were made and sold, so as to attract bird-life to the community; toll-gates were abolished along the two main arteries of travel; the removal of all telegraph and telephone poles was be-gun; an efficient Boy Scout troop was organized, and an American Legion post; the automobile speed limit was reduced from twenty-four to fifteen miles as a protection to children; roads were regularly swept, cleaned, and oiled, and uniform sidewalks advocated and secured.

Within seven years so efficiently had the Association functioned that its work attracted attention far beyond the immediate neighborhood of Philadelphia, and caused Theodore Roosevelt voluntarily to select it as a subject for a special magazine article in which he declared it to "stand as a model in civic matters." To-day it may be conservatively said of The Merion Civic Association that it is pointed out as one of the most successful suburban civic efforts in the country; as Doctor Lyman Abbott said in *The Outlook*, it has made "Merion a model suburb,

THE DUTCH GRANDFATHER

Who each year planted trees on his island home and transformed the place into a bower
of leafy beauty—an example followed in America by Edward Bok

which may standardize ideal suburban life, certainly for Philadelphia, possibly for the United States."

When the armistice was signed in November, 1918, the Association immediately canvassed the neighborhood to erect a suitable Tribute House, as a memorial to the eighty-three Merion boys who had gone into the Great War: a public building which would comprise a community centre, with an American Legion Post room, a Boy Scout house, an auditorium, and a meeting-place for the civic activities of Merion. A subscription was raised, and plans were already drawn for the Tribute House, when Mr. Eldridge R. Johnson, president of the Victor Talking Machine Company, one of the strong supporters of The Merion Civic Association, presented his entire estate of twelve acres, the finest in Merion, to the community, and agreed to build a Tribute House at his own expense. The grounds represented a gift of two hundred thousand dollars, and the building a gift of two hundred and fifty thousand dollars. This building, now about to be erected, will be one of the most beautiful and complete community centres in the United States.

Perhaps no other suburban civic effort proves the efficiency of community co-operation so well as does the seven years' work of The Merion Civic Association. It is a practical demonstration of what a community can do for itself by concerted action. It preached, from the very start, the gospel of united service; it translated into actual practice the doctrine of being one's brother's keeper, and it taught the invaluable habit of collective action. The Association has no legal powers; it rules solely by persuasion; it accomplishes by the power of combination; by a spirit of the community for the community.

When The Merion Civic Association was conceived, the

spirit of local pride was seemingly not present in the community. As a matter of fact, it was there as it is in practically every neighborhood; it was simply dormant; it had to be awakened, and its value brought vividly to the community consciousness.

CHAPTER XVI

When the virile figure of Theodore Roosevelt swung down the national highway, Bok was one of thousands of young men who felt strongly the attraction of his personality. Colonel Roosevelt was only five years the senior of the editor; he spoke, therefore, as one of his own years. The energy with which he said and did things appealed to Bok. He made Americanism something more real, more stirring than Bok had ever felt it; he explained national questions in a way that caught Bok's fancy and came within his comprehension. Bok's lines had been cast with many of the great men of the day, but he felt that there was something distinctive about the personality of this man: his method of doing things and his way of saying things. Bok observed everything Colonel Roosevelt did and read everything he wrote.

The editor now sought an opportunity to know personally the man whom he admired. It came at a dinner at the University Club, and Colonel Roosevelt suggested that they meet there the following day for a "talk-fest." For three hours the two talked together. The fact that Colonel Roosevelt was of Dutch ancestry interested Bok; that Bok was actually of Dutch birth made a strong appeal to the Colonel. With his tremendous breadth of interests, Roosevelt, Bok found, had followed him quite closely in his work, and was familiar with "its high points," as he called them. "We must work for the same ends,"

147

said the Colonel, "you in your way, I in mine. But our
lines are bound to cross. You and I can each become good
Americans by giving our best to make America better.
With the Dutch stock there is in both of us, there's no
limit to what we can do. Let's go to it." Naturally that
talk left the two firm friends.

Bok felt somehow that he had been given a new draft
of Americanism; the word took on a new meaning for him;
it stood for something different, something deeper and
finer than before. And every subsequent talk with Roosevelt deepened the feeling and stirred Bok's deepest ambitions. "Go to it, you Dutchman," Roosevelt would say,
and Bok *would* go to it. A talk with Roosevelt always left
him feeling as if mountains were the easiest things in the
world to move.

One of Theodore Roosevelt's arguments which made a
deep impression upon Bok was that no man had a right to
devote his entire life to the making of money. "You are
in a peculiar position," said the man of Oyster Bay one
day to Bok; "you are in that happy position where you
can make money and do good at the same time. A man
wields a tremendous power for good or for evil who is welcomed into a million homes and read with confidence.
That's fine, and is all right so far as it goes, and in your
case it goes very far. Still, there remains more for you to
do. The public has built up for you a personality: now
give that personality to whatever interests you in contact
with your immediate fellow-men: something in your neighborhood, your city, or your State. With one hand work
and write to your national audience: let no fads sway
you. Hew close to the line. But, with the other hand,
swing into the life immediately around you. Think it
over."

Bok did think it over. He was now realizing the dream
of his life for which he had worked: his means were sufficient to give his mother every comfort; to install her in
the most comfortable surroundings wherever she chose to
live; to make it possible for her to spend the winters in
the United States and the summers in the Netherlands,
and thus to keep in touch with her family and friends in
both countries. He had for years toiled unceasingly to
reach this point: he felt he had now achieved at least one
goal.

He had now turned instinctively to the making of a
home for himself. After an engagement of four years he
had been married, on October 22, 1896, to Mary Louise
Curtis, the only child of Mr. and Mrs. Cyrus H. K. Curtis;
two sons had been born to them; he had built and was occupying a house at Merion, Pennsylvania, a suburb six miles
from the Philadelphia City Hall. When she was in this
country his mother lived with him, and also his brother,
and, with a strong belief in life insurance, he had seen to
it that his family was provided for in case of personal incapacity or of his demise. In other words, he felt that he
had put his own house in order; he had carried out what
he felt is every man's duty: to be, first of all, a careful and
adequate provider for his family. He was now at the
point where he could begin to work for another goal, the
goal that he felt so few American men saw: the point in
his life where he could retire from the call of duty and
follow the call of inclination.

At the age of forty he tried to look ahead and plan out
his life as far as he could. Barring unforeseen obstacles,
he determined to retire from active business when he
reached his fiftieth year, and give the remainder of his life
over to those interests and influences which he assumed

now as part of his life, and which, at fifty, should seem to him best worth while. He realized that in order to do this he must do two things: he must husband his financial resources and he must begin to accumulate a mental reserve.

The wide public acceptance of the periodical which he edited naturally brought a share of financial success to him. He had experienced poverty, and as he subsequently wrote, in an article called "Why I Believe in Poverty," he was deeply grateful for his experience. He had known what it was to be poor; he had seen others dear to him suffer for the bare necessities; there was, in fact, not a single step on that hard road that he had not travelled. He could, therefore, sympathize with the fullest understanding with those similarly situated, could help as one who knew from practice and not from theory. He realized what a marvellous blessing poverty can be; but as a condition to experience, to derive from it poignant lessons, and then to get out of; not as a condition to stay in.

Of course many said to Bok when he wrote the article in which he expressed these beliefs: "That's all very well; easy enough to say, but how can you get out of it?" Bok realized that he could not definitely show any one the way. No one had shown him. No two persons can find the same way out. Bok determined to lift himself out of poverty because his mother was not born in it, did not belong in it, and could not stand it. That gave him the first essential: a purpose. Then he backed up the purpose with effort and an ever-ready willingness to work, and to work at anything that came his way, no matter what it was, so long as it meant "the way out." He did not pick and choose; he took what came, and did it in the best way he knew how; and when he did not like what he was doing he still did it as well as he could while he was doing it, but always with an eye single to the purpose not to do it any longer than was strictly necessary. He used every rung in the ladder as a rung to the one above. He always gave more than his particular position or salary asked for. He never worked by the clock; always by the job; and saw that it was well done regardless of the time it took to do it. This meant effort, of course, untiring, ceaseless, unsparing; and it meant work, hard as nails.

He was particularly careful never to live up to his income; and as his income increased he increased not the percentage of expenditure but the percentage of saving. Thrift was, of course, inborn with him as a Dutchman, but the necessity for it as a prime factor in life was burned into him by his experience with poverty. But he interpreted thrift not as a trait of niggardliness, but as Theodore Roosevelt interpreted it: common sense applied to spending.

At forty, therefore, he felt he had learned the first essential to carrying out his idea of retirement at fifty.

The second essential—varied interests outside of his business upon which he could rely on relinquishing his duties—he had not cultivated. He had quite naturally, in line with his belief that concentration means success, immersed himself in his business to the exclusion of almost everything else. He felt that he could now spare a certain percentage of his time to follow Theodore Roosevelt's ideas and let the breezes of other worlds blow over him. In that way he could do as Roosevelt suggested and as Bok now firmly believed was right: he could develop himself along broader lines, albeit the lines of his daily work were broadening in and of themselves, and he could so develop a new set of inner resources upon which he could draw when the time came to relinquish his editorial position.

He saw, on every side, the pathetic figures of men who

could not let go after their greatest usefulness was past; of other men who dropped before they realized their arrival at the end of the road; and, most pathetic of all, of men who having retired, but because of lack of inner resources did not know what to do with themselves, had become a trial to themselves, their families, and their communities.

Bok decided that, given health and mental freshness, he would say good-by to his public before his public might decide to say good-by to him. So, at forty, he candidly faced the facts of life and began to prepare himself for his retirement at fifty under circumstances that would be of his own making and not those of others.

And thereby Edward Bok proved that he was still, by instinct, a Dutchman, and had not in his thirty-four years of residence in the United States become so thoroughly Americanized as he believed.

However, it was an American, albeit of Dutch extraction, one whom he believed to be the greatest American in his own day, who had set him thinking and shown him the way.

CHAPTER XVII

One of the incidents connected with Edward Bok that Theodore Roosevelt never forgot was when Bok's eldest boy chose the Colonel as a Christmas present. And no incident better portrays the wonderful character of the Colonel than did his remarkable response to the compliment.

A vicious attack of double pneumonia had left the heart of the boy very weak—and Christmas was close by! So the father said:

"It's a quiet Christmas for you this year, boy. Suppose you do this: think of the one thing in the world that you would rather have than anything else and I'll give you that, and that will have to be your Christmas."

"I know now," came the instant reply.

"But the world is a big place, and there are lots of things in it, you know."

"I know that," said the boy, "but this is something I have wanted for a long time, and would rather have than anything else in the world." And he looked as if he meant it.

"Well, out with it, then, if you're so sure."

And to the father's astonished ears came this request:

"Take me to Washington as soon as my heart is all right, introduce me to President Roosevelt, and let me shake hands with him."

"All right," said the father, after recovering from his surprise. "I'll see whether I can fix it." And that morn-

153

ing a letter went to the President saying that he had been chosen as a Christmas present. Naturally, any man would have felt pleased, no matter how high his station, and for Theodore Roosevelt, father of boys, the message had a special appeal.

The letter had no sooner reached Washington than back came an answer, addressed not to the father but to the boy! It read:

> The White House, Washington.
> November 13th, 1907.
>
> DEAR CURTIS:
> Your father has just written me, and I want him to bring you on and shake hands with me as soon as you are well enough to travel. Then I am going to give you, myself, a copy of the book containing my hunting trips since I have been President; unless you will wait until the new edition, which contains two more chapters, is out. If so, I will send it to you, as this new edition probably won't be ready when you come on here.
> Give my warm regards to your father and mother.
> Sincerely yours,
> THEODORE ROOSEVELT.

Here was joy serene! But the boy's heart had acted queerly for a few days, and so the father wrote, thanked the President, and said that as soon as the heart moderated a bit the letter would be given the boy. It was a rare bit of consideration that now followed. No sooner had the father's letter reached the White House than an answer came back by first post—this time with a special-delivery stamp on it. It was Theodore Roosevelt, the father, who wrote this time; his mind and time filled with affairs of state, and yet full of tender thoughtfulness for a little boy:

Dear Mr. Bok:—

I have your letter of the 16th instant. I hope the little fellow will soon be all right. Instead of giving him my letter, give him a message from me based on the letter, if that will be better for him. Tell Mrs. Bok how deeply Mrs. Roosevelt and I sympathize with her. We know just how she feels.

Sincerely yours,

Theodore Roosevelt.

"That's pretty fine consideration," said the father. He got the letter during a business conference and he read it aloud to the group of business men. Some there were in that group who keenly differed with the President on national issues, but they were all fathers, and two of the sturdiest turned and walked to the window as they said: "Yes, that *is* fine!"

Then came the boy's pleasure when he was handed the letter; the next few days were spent inditing an answer to "my friend, the President." At last the momentous epistle seemed satisfactory, and off to the busy presidential desk went the boyish note, full of thanks and assurances that he would come just as soon as he could, and that Mr. Roosevelt must not get impatient!

The "soon as he could" time, however, did not come as quickly as all had hoped!—a little heart pumped for days full of oxygen and accelerated by hypodermic injections is slow to mend. But the President's framed letter, hanging on the spot on the wall first seen in the morning, was a daily consolation.

Then, in March, although four months after the promise—and it would not have been strange, in his busy life, for the President to have forgotten or at least overlooked it—on the very day that the book was published came a special "large-paper" copy of *The Outdoor Pastimes*

of an American Hunter, and on the fly-leaf there greeted
the boy, in the President's own hand:

To MASTER CURTIS BOK,
    With the best wishes of his friend,
                                THEODORE ROOSEVELT.
    March 11, 1908.

The boy's cup was now full, and so said his letter
to the President. And the President wrote back to the
father: "I am really immensely amused and interested,
and shall be mighty glad to see the little fellow."

In the spring, on a beautiful May day, came the great
moment. The mother had to go along, the boy insisted,
to see the great event, and so the trio found themselves
shaking the hand of the President's secretary at the White
House.

"Oh, the President is looking for you, all right," he
said to the boy, and then the next moment the three were
in a large room. Mr. Roosevelt, with beaming face, was
already striding across the room, and with a "Well, well,
and so this is my friend Curtis!" the two stood looking
into each other's faces, each fairly wreathed in smiles,
and each industriously shaking the hand of the other.

"Yes, Mr. President, I'm mighty glad to see you!"
said the boy.

"I am glad to see you, Curtis," returned Mr. Roosevelt.

Then there came a white rose from the presidential
desk for the mother, but after that father and mother
might as well have faded away. Nobody existed save
the President and the boy. The anteroom was full; in
the Cabinet-room a delegation waited to be addressed.
But affairs of state were at a complete standstill as, with

boyish zeal, the President became oblivious to all but the boy before him.

"Now, Curtis, I've got some pictures here of bears that a friend of mine has just shot. Look at that whopper, fifteen hundred pounds—that's as much as a horse weighs, you know. Now, my friend shot him"—and it was a toss-up who was the more keenly interested, the real boy or the man-boy, as picture after picture came out and bear adventure crowded upon the heels of bear adventure.

"Gee, he's a corker, all right!" came from the boy at one point, and then, from the President: "That's right, he *is* a corker. Now you see his head here"—and then both were off again.

The private secretary came in at this point and whispered in the President's ear.

"I know, I know. I'll see him later. Say that I am very busy now." And the face beamed with smiles.

"Now, Mr. President—" began the father.

"No, sir; no, sir; not at all. Affairs can wait. This is a long-standing engagement between Curtis and me, and that must come first. Isn't that so, Curtis?"

Of course the boy agreed.

Suddenly the boy looked around the room and said: "Where's your gun, Mr. President? Got it here?"

"No," laughingly came from the President, "but I'll tell you"—and then the two heads were together again.

A moment for breath-taking came, and the boy said: "Aren't you ever afraid of being shot?"

"You mean while I am hunting?"

"Oh, no. I mean as President."

"No," replied the smiling President. "I'll tell you, Curtis; I'm too busy to think about that. I have too many things to do to bother about anything of that sort.

When I was in battle I was always too anxious to get to the front to think about the shots. And here—well, here I'm too busy too. Never think about it. But I'll tell you, Curtis, there are some men down there," pointing out of the window in the direction of the capitol, "called the Congress, and if they would only give me the four battleships I want, I'd be perfectly willing to have any one take a crack at me." Then, for the first time recognizing the existence of the parents, the President said: "And I don't know but if they did pick me off I'd be pretty well ahead of the game."

Just in that moment only did the boy-knowing President get a single inch above the boy-interest. It was astonishing to see the natural accuracy with which the man gauged the boy-level.

"Now, how would you like to see a bear, Curtis?" came next. "I know where there's a beauty, twelve hundred pounds."

"Must be some bear!" interjected the boy.

"That's what it is," put in the President. "Regular cinnamon-brown type"—and then off went the talk to the big bear at the Washington "Zoo" where the President was to send the boy.

Then, after a little: "Now, Curtis, see those men over there in that room. They've travelled from all parts of the country to come here at my invitation, and I've got to make a little speech to them, and I'll do that while you go off to see the bear."

And then the hand came forth to say good-by. The boy put his in it, each looked into the other's face, and on neither was there a place big enough to put a ten-cent piece that was not wreathed in smiles. "He certainly is all right," said the boy to the father, looking wistfully after the President.

Almost to the other room had the President gone when he, too, instinctively looked back to find the boy following him with his eyes. He stopped, wheeled around, and then the two instinctively sought each other again. The President came back, the boy went forward. This time each held out both hands, and as each looked once more into the other's eyes a world of complete understanding was in both faces, and every looker-on smiled with them.

"Good-by, Curtis," came at last from the President.

"Good-by, Mr. President," came from the boy.

Then, with another pump-handly shake and with a "Gee, but he's great, all right!" the boy went out to see the cinnamon-bear at the "Zoo," and to live it all over in the days to come.

Two boy-hearts had met, although one of them belonged to the President of the United States.

CHAPTER XVIII

ADVENTURES IN MUSIC

One of the misfortunes of Edward Bok's training, which he realized more clearly as time went on, was that music had little or no place in his life. His mother did not play; and aside from the fact that his father and mother were patrons of the opera during their residence in The Netherlands, the musical atmosphere was lacking in his home. He realized how welcome an outlet music might be in his now busy life. So what he lacked himself and realized as a distinct omission in his own life he decided to make possible for others.

The Ladies' Home Journal began to strike a definite musical note. It first caught the eye and ear of its public by presenting the popular new marches by John Philip Sousa; and when the comic opera of "Robin Hood" became the favorite of the day, it secured all the new compositions by Reginald de Koven. Following these, it introduced its readers to new compositions by Sir Arthur Sullivan, Tosti, Moszkowski, Richard Strauss, Paderewski, Josef Hofmann, Edouard Strauss, and Mascagni. Bok induced Josef Hofmann to give a series of piano lessons in his magazine, and Madame Marchesi a series of vocal lessons. *The Journal* introduced its readers to all the great instrumental and vocal artists of the day through articles; it offered prizes for the best piano and vocal compositions; it had the leading critics of New York, Boston, and Chicago write articles explanatory of orchestral music and how to listen to music.

Bok was early attracted by the abilities of Josef Hofmann. In 1898, he met the pianist, who was then twenty-two years old. Of his musical ability Bok could not judge, but he was much impressed by his unusual mentality, and soon both learned and felt that Hofmann's art was deeply and firmly rooted. Hofmann had a wider knowledge of affairs than other musicians whom Bok had met; he had not narrowed his interests to his own art. He was striving to achieve a position in his art, and, finding that he had literary ability, Bok asked him to write a reminiscent article on his famous master, Rubinstein.

This was followed by other articles; the publication of his new mazurka; still further articles; and then, in 1907, Bok offered him a regular department in the magazine and a salaried editorship on his staff.

Bok's musical friends and the music critics tried to convince the editor that Hofmann's art lay not so deep as Bok imagined; that he had been a child prodigy, and would end where all child prodigies invariably end—opinions which make curious reading now in view of Hofmann's commanding position in the world of music. But while Bok lacked musical knowledge, his instinct led him to adhere to his belief in Hofmann; and for twelve years, until Bok's retirement as editor, the pianist was a regular contributor to the magazine. His success was, of course, unquestioned. He answered hundreds of questions sent him by his readers, and these answers furnished such valuable advice for piano students that two volumes were made in book form and are to-day used by piano teachers and students as authoritative guides.

Meanwhile, Bok's marriage had brought music directly into his domestic circle. Mrs. Bok loved music, was a pianist herself, and sought to acquaint her husband with what his former training had omitted. Hofmann and Bok had become strong friends outside of the editorial relation, and the pianist frequently visited the Bok home. But it was some time, even with these influences surrounding him, before music began to play any real part in Bok's own life.

He attended the opera occasionally; more or less under protest, because of its length, and because his mind was too practical for the indirect operatic form. He could not remain patient at a recital; the effort to listen to one performer for an hour and a half was too severe a tax upon his restless nature. The Philadelphia Orchestra gave a symphony concert each Saturday evening, and Bok dreaded the coming of that evening in each week for fear of being taken to hear music which he was convinced was "over his head."

Like many men of his practical nature, he had made up his mind on this point without ever having heard such a concert. The word "symphony" was enough; it conveyed to him a form of the highest music quite beyond his comprehension. Then, too, in the back of his mind there was the feeling that, while he was perfectly willing to offer the best that the musical world afforded in his magazine, his readers were primarily women, and the appeal of music, after all, he felt was largely, if not wholly, to the feminine nature. It was very satisfying to him to hear his wife play in the evening; but when it came to public concerts, they were not for his masculine nature. In other words, Bok shared the all too common masculine notion that music is for women and has little place in the lives of men.

One day Josef Hofmann gave Bok an entirely new point of view. The artist was rehearsing in Philadelphia for an appearance with the orchestra, and the pianist was telling

Bok and his wife of the desire of Leopold Stokowski, who
had recently become conductor of the Philadelphia Orchestra, to eliminate encores from his symphonic programmes;
he wanted to begin the experiment with Hofmann's appearance that week. This was a novel thought to Bok: why
eliminate encores from any concert? If he liked the way
any performer played, he had always done his share to
secure an encore. Why should not the public have an encore if it desired it, and why should a conductor or a performer object? Hofmann explained to him the entity of
a symphonic programme; that it was made up with one
composition in relation to the others as a sympathetic
unit, and that an encore was an intrusion, disturbing the
harmony of the whole.

"I wish you would let Stokowski come out and explain
to you what he is trying to do," said Hofmann. "He
knows what he wants, and he is right in his efforts; but
he doesn't know how to educate the public. There is
where you could help him."

But Bok had no desire to meet Stokowski. He mentally pictured the conductor: long hair; feet never touching
the earth; temperament galore; he knew them! And he
had no wish to introduce the type into his home life.

Mrs. Bok, however, ably seconded Josef Hofmann,
and endeavored to dissipate Bok's preconceived notion,
with the result that Stokowski came to the Bok home.

Bok was not slow to see Stokowski was quite the reverse of his mental picture, and became intensely interested
in the youthful conductor's practical way of looking at
things. It was agreed that the encore "bull" was to be
taken by the horns that week; that no matter what the
ovation to Hofmann might be, however the public might
clamor, no encore was to be forthcoming; and Bok was to

give the public an explanation during the following week. The next concert was to present Mischa Elman, and his co-operation was assured so that continuity of effort might be counted upon.

In order to have first-hand information, Bok attended the concert that Saturday evening. The symphony, Dvořák's "New World Symphony," amazed Bok by its beauty; he was more astonished that he could so easily grasp any music in symphonic form. He was equally surprised at the simple beauty of the other numbers on the programme, and wondered not a little at his own perfectly absorbed attention during Hofmann's playing of a rather long concerto.

The pianist's performance was so beautiful that the audience was uproarious in its approval; it had calculated, of course, upon an encore, and recalled the pianist again and again until he had appeared and bowed his thanks several times. But there was no encore; the stage hands appeared and moved the piano to one side, and the audience relapsed into unsatisfied and rather bewildered silence.

Then followed Bok's publicity work in the newspapers, beginning the next day, exonerating Hofmann and explaining the situation. The following week, with Mischa Elman as soloist, the audience once more tried to have its way and its cherished encore, but again none was forthcoming. Once more the newspapers explained; the battle was won, and the no-encore rule has prevailed at the Philadelphia Orchestra concerts from that day to this, with the public entirely resigned to the idea and satisfied with the reason therefor.

But the bewildered Bok could not make out exactly what had happened to his preconceived notion about symphonic music. He attended the following Saturday evening concert; listened to a Brahms symphony that pleased him even more than had "The New World," and when, two weeks later, he heard the Tschaikowski "Pathetique" and later the "Unfinished" symphony, by Schubert, and a Beethoven symphony, attracted by each in turn, he realized that his prejudice against the whole question of symphonic music had been both wrongly conceived and baseless.

He now began to see the possibility of a whole world of beauty which up to that time had been closed to him, and he made up his mind that he would enter it. Somehow or other, he found the appeal of music did not confine itself to women; it seemed to have a message for men. Then, too, instead of dreading the approach of Saturday evenings, he was looking forward to them, and invariably so arranged his engagements that they might not interfere with his attendance at the orchestra concerts.

After a busy week, he discovered that nothing he had ever experienced served to quiet him so much as these end-of-the-week concerts. They were not too long, an hour and a half at the utmost; and, above all, except now and then, when the conductor would take a flight into the world of Bach, he found he followed him with at least a moderate degree of intelligence; certainly with personal pleasure and inner satisfaction.

Bok concluded he would not read the articles he had published on the meaning of the different "sections" of a symphony orchestra, or the books issued on that subject. He would try to solve the mechanism of an orchestra, for himself, and ascertain as he went along the relation that each portion bore to the other. When, therefore, in 1913, the president of the Philadelphia Orchestra Association asked him to become a member of its Board of Directors, his acceptance was a natural step in the gradual development of his interest in orchestral music.

The public support given to orchestras now greatly interested Bok. He was surprised to find that every symphony orchestra had a yearly deficit. This he immediately attributed to faulty management; but on investigating the whole question he learned that a symphony orchestra could not possibly operate, at a profit or even on a self-sustaining basis, because of its weekly change of programme, the incessant rehearsals required, and the limited number of times it could actually play within a contracted season. An annual deficit was inevitable.

He found that the Philadelphia Orchestra had a small but faithful group of guarantors who each year made good the deficit in addition to paying for its concert seats. This did not seem to Bok a sound business plan; it made of the orchestra a necessarily exclusive organization, maintained by a few; and it gave out this impression to the general public, which felt that it did not "belong," whereas the true relation of public and orchestra was that of mutual dependence. Other orchestras, he found, as, for example, the Boston Symphony and the New York Philharmonic had their deficits met by one individual patron in each case. This, to Bok's mind, was an even worse system, since it entirely excluded the public, making the orchestra dependent on the continued interest and life of a single man.

In 1916 Bok sought Mr. Alexander Van Rensselaer, the president of the Philadelphia Orchestra Association, and proposed that he, himself, should guarantee the deficit of the orchestra for five years, provided that during that period an endowment fund should be raised, contributed by a large number of subscribers, and sufficient in amount to meet, from its interest, the annual deficit. It was agreed that the donor should remain in strict anonymity, an understanding which has been adhered to until the present writing.

The offer from the "anonymous donor," presented by the president, was accepted by the Orchestra Association. A subscription to an endowment fund was shortly afterward begun; and the amount had been brought to eight hundred thousand dollars when the Great War interrupted any further additions. In the autumn of 1919, however, a city-wide campaign for an addition of one million dollars to the endowment fund was launched. The amount was not only secured, but oversubscribed. Thus, instead of a guarantee fund, contributed by thirteen hundred subscribers, with the necessity for annual collection, an endowment fund of one million eight hundred thousand dollars, contributed by fourteen thousand subscribers, has been secured; and the Philadelphia Orchestra has been promoted from a privately maintained organization to a public institution in which fourteen thousand residents of Philadelphia feel a proprietary interest. It has become in fact, as well as in name, "our orchestra."

CHAPTER XIX

The success of *The Ladies' Home Journal* went steadily forward. The circulation had passed the previously unheard-of figure for a monthly magazine of a million and a half copies per month; it had now touched a million and three-quarters.

And not only was the figure so high, but the circulation itself was absolutely free from "water." The public could not obtain the magazine through what are known as clubbing-rates, since no subscriber was permitted to include any other magazine with it; years ago it had abandoned the practice of offering premiums or consideration of any kind to induce subscriptions; and the newsdealers were not allowed to return unsold copies of the periodical. Hence every copy was either purchased by the public at the full price at a news stand, or subscribed for at its stated subscription price. It was, in short, an authoritative circulation. And on every hand the question was being asked: "How is it done? How is such a high circulation obtained?"

Bok's invariable answer was that he gave his readers the very best of the class of reading that he believed would interest them, and that he spared neither effort nor expense to obtain it for them. When Mr. Howells once asked him how he classified his audience, Bok replied: "We appeal to the intelligent American woman rather than to the intellectual type." And he gave her the best he could obtain. As he knew her to be fond of the personal type of literature, he gave her in succession Jane Addams's story of "My Fifteen Years at Hull House," and the remarkable

narration of Helen Keller's "Story of My Life"; he invited
Henry Van Dyke, who had never been in the Holy Land,
to go there, camp out in a tent, and then write a series of
sketches, "Out of Doors in the Holy Land"; he induced
Lyman Abbott to tell the story of "My Fifty Years as a
Minister." He asked Gene Stratton Porter to tell of her
bird-experiences in the series: "What I Have Done with
Birds"; he persuaded Dean Hodges to turn from his work
of training young clergymen at the Episcopal Seminary,
at Cambridge, and write one of the most successful series
of Bible stories for children ever printed; and then he supplemented this feature for children by publishing Rudyard
Kipling's "Just So" stories and his "Puck of Pook's Hill."
He induced F. Hopkinson Smith to tell the best stories he
had ever heard in his wide travels in "The Man in the Arm
Chair"; he got Kate Douglas Wiggin to tell a country
church experience of hers in "The Old Peabody Pew"; and
Jean Webster her knowledge of almshouse life in "Daddy
Long Legs."

The readers of *The Ladies' Home Journal* realized that
it searched the whole field of endeavor in literature and art
to secure what would interest them, and they responded
with their support.

Another of Bok's methods in editing was to do the
common thing in an uncommon way. He had the faculty
of putting old wine in new bottles and the public liked it.
His ideas were not new; he knew there were no new ideas,
but he presented his ideas in such a way that they seemed
new. It is a significant fact, too, that a large public will
respond more quickly to an idea than it will to a name.

When, early in 1917, events began so to shape themselves as directly to point to the entrance of the United

States into the Great War, Edward Bok set himself to formulate a policy for *The Ladies' Home Journal.* He knew that he was in an almost insurmountably difficult position. The huge edition necessitated going to press fully six weeks in advance of publication, and the preparation of material fully four weeks previous to that. He could not, therefore, get much closer than ten weeks to the date when his readers received the magazine. And he knew that events, in war time, had a way of moving rapidly.

Late in January he went to Washington, consulted those authorities who could indicate possibilities to him better than any one else, and found, as he had suspected, that the entry of the United States into the war was a practical certainty; it was only a question of time.

Bok went South for a month's holiday to get ready for the fray, and in the saddle and on the golf links he formulated a policy. The newspapers and weeklies would send innumerable correspondents to the front, and obviously, with the necessity for going to press so far in advance, *The Journal* could not compete with them. They would depict every activity in the field. There was but one logical thing for him to do: ignore the "front" entirely, refuse all the offers of correspondents, men and women, who wanted to go with the armies for his magazine, and cover fully and practically the results of the war as they would affect the women left behind. He went carefully over the ground to see what these would be, along what particular lines women's activities would be most likely to go, and then went back to Washington.

It was now March. He conferred with the President, had his fears confirmed, and offered all the resources of his magazine to the government. His diagnosis of the situation was verified in every detail by the authorities whom he consulted. *The Ladies' Home Journal* could best serve by keeping up the morale at home and by helping to meet the problems that would confront the women; as the President said: "Give help in the second line of defense."

A year before, Bok had opened a separate editorial office in Washington and had secured Dudley Harmon, the Washington correspondent for the *New York Sun*, as his editor-in-charge. The purpose was to bring the women of the country into a clearer understanding of their government and a closer relation with it. This work had been so successful as to necessitate a force of four offices and twenty stenographers. Bok now placed this Washington office on a war-basis, bringing it into close relation with every department of the government that would be connected with the war activities. By this means, he had an editor and an organized force on the spot, devoting full time to the preparation of war material, with Mr. Harmon in daily conference with the department chiefs to secure the newest developments.

Bok learned that the country's first act would be to recruit for the navy, so as to get this branch of the service into a state of preparedness. He therefore secured Franklin D. Roosevelt, assistant secretary of the navy, to write an article explaining to mothers why they should let their boys volunteer for the Navy and what it would mean to them.

He made arrangements at the American Red Cross Headquarters for an official department to begin at once in the magazine, telling women the first steps that would be taken by the Red Cross and how they could help. He secured former President William Howard Taft, as chairman of the Central Committee of the Red Cross, for the editor of this department.

He cabled to Viscount Northcliffe and Ian Hay for articles showing what the English women had done at the outbreak of the war, the mistakes they had made, what errors the American women should avoid, the right lines along which English women had worked and how their American sisters could adapt these methods to transatlantic conditions.

And so it happened that when the first war issue of *The Journal* appeared on April 20th, only three weeks after the President's declaration, it was the only monthly that recognized the existence of war, and its pages had already begun to indicate practical lines along which women could help.

The editor had been told that the question of food would come to be of paramount importance; he knew that Herbert Hoover had been asked to return to America as soon as he could close his work abroad, and he cabled over to his English representative to arrange that the proposed Food Administrator should know, at first hand, of the magazine and its possibilities for the furtherance of the proposed Food Administration work.

The Food Administration was no sooner organized than Bok made arrangements for an authoritative department to be conducted in his magazine, reflecting the plans and desires of the Food Administration, and Herbert Hoover's first public declaration to the women of America as food administrator was published in *The Ladies' Home Journal.* Bok now placed all the resources of his four-color press-work at Mr. Hoover's disposal; and the Food Administration's domestic experts, in conjunction with the full culinary staff of the magazine, prepared the new war dishes and presented them appetizingly in full colors under the personal endorsement of Mr. Hoover and the Food Administration. From six to sixteen articles per month were now coming from Mr. Hoover's department alone.

Secretary of the Treasury McAdoo interpreted the first Liberty Loan "drive" to the women; the President of the United States, in a special message to women, wrote in behalf of the subsequent Loan; Bernard Baruch, as chairman of the War Industries Board, made clear the need for war-time thrift; the recalled ambassador to Germany, James W. Gerard, told of the ingenious plans resorted to by German women which American women could profitably copy; and Elizabeth, Queen of the Belgians, explained the plight of the babies and children of Belgium, and made a plea to the women of the magazine to help. So straight to the point did the Queen write, and so well did she present her case that within six months there had been sent to her, through *The Ladies' Home Journal*, two hundred and forty-eight thousand cans of condensed milk, seventy-two thousand cans of pork and beans, five thousand cans of infants' prepared food, eighty thousand cans of beef soup, and nearly four thousand bushels of wheat, purchased with the money donated by the magazine readers.

Considering the difficulties to be surmounted, due to the advance preparation of material, and considering that, at the best, most of its advance information, even by the highest authorities, could only be in the nature of surmise, the comprehensive manner in which *The Ladies' Home Journal* covered every activity of women during the Great War, will always remain one of the magazine's most noteworthy achievements. This can be said without reserve here, since the credit is due to no single person; it was the combined, careful work of its entire staff, weighing every step before it was taken, looking as clearly into the future as circumstances made possible, and always seeking the most authoritative sources of information.

It was in the summer of 1918 that Edward Bok received from the British Government, through its department of public information, of which Lord Beaverbrook was the minister, an invitation to join a party of thirteen American editors to visit Great Britain and France. The British Government, not versed in publicity methods, was anxious that selected parties of American publicists should see, personally, what Great Britain had done, and was doing in the war; and it had decided to ask a few individuals to pay personal visits to its munition factories, its great aerodromes, its Great Fleet, which then lay in the Firth of Forth, and to the battle-fields. It was understood that no specific obligation rested upon any member of the party to write of what he saw: he was asked simply to observe and then, with discretion, use his observations for his own guidance and information in future writing. In fact, each member was explicitly told that much of what he would see could not be revealed either personally or in print.

The party embarked in August amid all the attendant secrecy of war conditions. The steamer was known only by a number, although later it turned out to be the White Star liner, *Adriatic*. Preceded by a powerful United States cruiser, flanked by destroyers, guided overhead by observation balloons, the *Adriatic* was found to be the first ship in a convoy of sixteen other ships with thirty thousand United States troops on board.

It was a veritable Armada that steamed out of lower New York harbor on that early August morning, headed straight into the rising sun. But it was a voyage of unpleasant war reminders, with life-savers carried every mo-

WHERE EDWARD BOK IS HAPPIEST: IN HIS GARDEN

ment of the day, with every light out at night, with every window and door as if hermetically sealed so that the stuffy cabins deprived of sleep those accustomed to fresh air, with over sixty army men and civilians on watch at night, with life-drills each day, with lessons as to behavior in life-boats; and with a fleet of eighteen British destroyers meeting the convoy upon its approach to the Irish Coast after a thirteen days' voyage of constant anxiety. No one could say he travelled across the Atlantic Ocean in war days for pleasure, and no one did.

Once ashore, the party began a series of inspections of munition plants, ship-yards, aeroplane factories and of meetings with the different members of the English War Cabinet. Luncheons and dinners were the order of each day until broken by a journey to Edinburgh to see the amazing Great Fleet, with the addition of six of the foremost fighting machines of the United States Navy, all straining like dogs at leash, awaiting an expected dash from the bottled-up German fleet. It was a formidable sight, perhaps never equalled: those lines of huge, menacing, and yet protecting fighting machines stretching down the river for miles, all conveying the single thought of the power and extent of the British Navy and its formidable character as a fighting unit.

It was upon his return to London that Bok learned, through the confidence of a member of the British "inner circle," the amazing news that the war was practically over: that Bulgaria had capitulated and was suing for peace; that two of the Central Power provinces had indicated their strong desire that the war should end; and that the first peace intimations had gone to the President of the United States. All diplomatic eyes were turned toward Washington. Yet not a hint of the impending events had reached the public. The Germans were being beaten back, that was known; it was evident that the morale of the German army was broken; that Foch had turned the tide toward victory; but even the best-informed military authorities outside of the inner diplomatic circles, predicted that the war would last until the spring of 1919, when a final "drive" would end it. Yet, at that very moment, the end of the war was in sight!

Next Bok went to France to visit the battle-fields. It was arranged that the party should first, under guidance of British officers, visit back of the British lines; and then, successively, be turned over to the American and French Governments, and visit the operations back of their armies.

It is an amusing fact that although each detail of officers delegated to escort the party "to the front" received the most explicit instructions from their superior officers to take the party only to the quiet sectors where there was no fighting going on, each detail from the three governments successively brought the party directly under shell-fire, and each on the first day of the "inspection." It was unconsciously done: the officers were as much amazed to find themselves under fire as were the members of the party, except that the latter did not feel the responsibility to an equal degree. The officers, in each case, were plainly worried: the editors were intensely interested.

They were depressing trips through miles and miles of devastated villages and small cities. From two to three days each were spent in front-line posts on the Amiens-Bethune, Albert-Peronne, Bapaume-Soissons, St. Mihiel, and back of the Argonne sectors. Often, the party was the first civilian group to enter a town evacuated only a week before, and all the horrible evidence of bloody warfare was fresh and plain. Bodies of German soldiers lay in the trenches where they had fallen; wired bombs were on every hand, so that no object could be touched that lay on the battle-fields; the streets of some of the towns were still mined, so that no automobiles could enter; the towns were deserted, the streets desolate. It was an appalling panorama of the most frightful results of war.

The picturesqueness and romance of the war of picture books were missing. To stand beside an English battery of thirty guns laying a barrage as they fired their shells to a point ten miles distant, made one feel as if one were an actual part of real warfare, and yet far removed from it, until the battery was located from the enemy's "sausage observation"; then the shells from the enemy fired a return salvo, and the better part of valor was discretion a few miles farther back.

Bok was standing talking to the commandant of one of the great French army supply depots one morning. He was a man of forty; a colonel in the regular French army. An erect, sturdy-looking man with white hair and mustache, and who wore the single star of a subaltern on his sleeve, came up, saluted, delivered a message, and then asked:

"Are there any more orders, sir?"

"No," was the reply.

He brought his heels together with a click, saluted again, and went away.

The commandant turned to Bok with a peculiar smile on his face and asked:

"Do you know who that man is?"

"No," was the reply.

"That is my father," was the answer.

The father was then exactly seventy-two years old. He was a retired business man when the war broke out.

After two years of the heroic struggle he decided that he couldn't keep out of it. He was too old to fight, but after long insistence he secured a commission. By one of the many curious coincidences of the war he was assigned to serve under his own son.

When under the most trying conditions, the Americans never lost their sense of fun. On the staff of a prison hospital in Germany, where a number of captured American soldiers were being treated, a German sergeant became quite friendly with the prisoners under his care. One day he told them that he had been ordered to active service on the front. He felt convinced that he would be captured by the English, and asked the Americans if they would not give him some sort of testimonial which he could show if he were taken prisoner, so that he would not be ill-treated.

The Americans were much amused at this idea, and concocted a note of introduction, written in English. The German sergeant knew no English and could not understand his testimonial, but he tucked it in his pocket, well satisfied.

In due time, he was sent to the front and was captured by "the ladies from hell," as the Germans called the Scotch kilties. He at once presented his introduction, and his captors laughed heartily when they read:

"This is L——. He is not a bad sort of chap. Don't shoot him; torture him slowly to death."

The amazing part of the "show," however, was the American doughboy. Never was there a more cheerful, laughing, good-natured set of boys in the world; never a more homesick, lonely, and complaining set. But good nature predominated, and the smile was always uppermost, even when the moment looked the blackest, the privations were worst, and the longing for home the deepest.

Bok had been talking to a boy who lived near his own home, who was on his way to the front and "over the top" in the Argonne mess. Three days afterward, at a hospital base where a hospital train was just discharging its load of wounded, Bok walked among the boys as they lay on their stretchers on the railroad platform waiting for bearers to carry them into the huts. As he approached one stretcher, a cheery voice called, "Hello, Mr. Bok. Here I am again."

It was the boy he had left just seventy-two hours before hearty and well.

"Well, my boy, you weren't in it long, were you?"

"No, sir," answered the boy; "Fritzie sure got me first thing. Hadn't gone a hundred yards over the top. Got a cigarette?" (the invariable question).

Bok handed a cigarette to the boy, who then said: "Mind sticking it in my mouth?" Bok did so and then offered him a light; the boy continued, all with his wonderful smile: "If you don't mind, would you just light it? You see, Fritzie kept both of my hooks as souvenirs."

With both arms amputated, the boy could still jest and smile!

It was the same boy who on his hospital cot the next day said: "Don't you think you could do something for the chap next to me, there on my left? He's really suffering: cried like hell all last night. It would be a Godsend if you could get Doc to do something."

A promise was given that the surgeon should be seen at once, but the boy was asked: "How about you?"

"Oh," came the cheerful answer, "I'm all right. I haven't anything to hurt. My wounded members are gone—just plain gone. But that chap has got something —he got the real thing!"

What was the real thing according to such a boy's idea?

Bok had had enough of war in all its aspects; he felt a sigh of relief when, a few days thereafter, he boarded *The Empress of Asia* for home, after a ten-weeks' absence. He hoped never again to see, at first hand, what war meant!

CHAPTER XX

THE THIRD PERIOD

On the voyage home, Edward Bok decided that, now the war was over, he would ask his company to release him from the editorship of *The Ladies' Home Journal.* His original plan had been to retire at the end of a quarter of a century of editorship, when in his fiftieth year. He was, therefore, six years behind his schedule. In October, 1919, he would reach his thirtieth anniversary as editor, and he fixed upon this as an appropriate time for the relinquishment of his duties.

He felt he had carried out the conditions under which the editorship of the magazine had been transferred to him by Mrs. Curtis, that he had brought them to fruition, and that any further carrying on of the periodical by him would be of a supplementary character. He had, too, realized his hope of helping to create a national institution of service to the American woman, and he felt that his part in the work was done.

He considered carefully where he would leave an institution which the public had so thoroughly associated with his personality, and he felt that at no point in its history could he so safely transfer it to other hands. The position of the magazine in the public estimation was unquestioned; it had never been so strong. Its circulation not only had outstripped that of any other monthly periodical, but it was still growing so rapidly that it was only a question of a few months when it would reach the

almost incredible mark of two million copies per month.
With its advertising patronage exceeding that of any other
monthly, the periodical had become, probably, the most
valuable and profitable piece of magazine property in the
world.

The time might never come again when all conditions
would be equally favorable to a change of editorship. The
position of the magazine was so thoroughly assured that
its progress could hardly be affected by the retirement of
one editor, and the accession of another. There was a
competent editorial staff, the members of which had been
with the periodical from ten to thirty years each. This
staff had been a very large factor in the success of the magazine. While Bok had furnished the initiative and supplied
the directing power, a large part of the editorial success of
the magazine was due to the staff. It could carry on the
magazine without his guidance.

Moreover, Bok wished to say good-by to his public
before it decided, for some reason or other, to say good-
by to him. He had no desire to outstay his welcome.
That public had been wonderfully indulgent toward his
shortcomings, lenient with his errors, and tremendously
inspiring to his best endeavor. He would not ask too much
of it. Thirty years was a long tenure of office, one of the
longest, in point of consecutively active editorship, in the
history of American magazines.

He had helped to create and to put into the life of the
American home a magazine of peculiar distinction. From
its beginning it had been unlike any other periodical; it
had always retained its individuality as a magazine apart
from the others. It had sought to be something more than
a mere assemblage of stories and articles. It had consistently stood for ideals; and, save in one or two instances, it

had carried through what it undertook to achieve. It had a record of worthy accomplishment; a more fruitful record than many imagined. It had become a national institution such as no other magazine had ever been. It was indisputably accepted by the public and by business interests alike as the recognized avenue of approach to the intelligent homes of America.

Edward Bok was content to leave it at this point.

He explained all this in December, 1918, to the Board of Directors, and asked that his resignation be considered. It was understood that he was to serve out his thirty years, thus remaining with the magazine for the best part of another year.

In the material which *The Journal* now included in its contents, it began to point the way to the problems which would face women during the reconstruction period. Bok scanned the rather crowded field of thought very carefully, and selected for discussion in the magazine such questions as seemed to him most important for the public to understand in order to face and solve its impending problems. The outstanding question he saw which would immediately face men and women of the country was the problem of Americanization. The war and its after-effects had clearly demonstrated this to be the most vital need in the life of the nation, not only for the foreign-born but for the American as well.

The more one studied the problem the clearer it became that the vast majority of American-born needed a refreshing, and, in many cases, a new conception of American ideals as much as did the foreign-born, and that the latter could never be taught what America and its institutions stood for until they were more clearly defined in the mind of the men and women of American birth.

Bok went to Washington, consulted with Franklin K. Lane, secretary of the interior, of whose department the Government Bureau of Americanization was a part. A comprehensive series of articles was outlined; the most expert writer, Esther Everett Lape, who had several years of actual experience in Americanization work, was selected; Secretary Lane agreed personally to read and pass upon the material, and to assume the responsibility for its publication.

With the full and direct co-operation of the Federal Bureau of Americanization, the material was assembled and worked up with the result that, in the opinion of the director of the Federal Bureau, the series proved to be the most comprehensive exposition of practical Americanization adapted to city, town, and village, thus far published.

The work on this series was one of the last acts of Edward Bok's editorship; and it was peculiarly gratifying to him that his editorial work should end with the exposition of that Americanization of which he himself was a product. It seemed a fitting close to the career of a foreign-born Americanized editor.

The scope of the reconstruction articles now published, and the clarity of vision shown in the selection of the subjects, gave a fresh impetus to the circulation of the magazine; and now that the government's embargo on the use of paper had been removed, the full editions of the periodical could again be printed. The public responded instantly.

The result reached phenomenal figures. The last number under Bok's full editorial control was the issue of October, 1919. This number was oversold with a printed edition of two million copies—a record never before achieved by any magazine. This same issue presented another

record unattained in any single number of any periodical
in the world. It carried between its covers the amazing
total of over one million dollars in advertisements.

This was the psychological point at which to stop.
And Edward Bok did. Although his official relation as
editor did not terminate until January, 1920, when the
number which contained his valedictory editorial was
issued, his actual editorship ceased on September 22, 1919.
On that day he handed over the reins to his successor.

The announcement of Edward Bok's retirement came
as a great surprise to his friends. Save for one here and
there, who had a clearer vision, the feeling was general
that he had made a mistake. He was fifty-six, in the
prime of life, never in better health, with "success lying
easily upon him"—said one; "at the very summit of his
career," said another—and all agreed it was "queer,"
"strange,"—unless, they argued, he was really ill. Even
the most acute students of human affairs among his friends
wondered. It seemed incomprehensible that any man
should want to give up before he was, for some reason,
compelled to do so. A man should go on until he "dropped
in the harness," they argued.

Bok agreed that any man had a perfect right to work
until he *did* "drop in the harness." But, he argued, if he
conceded this right to others, why should they not concede
to him the privilege of dropping with the blinders off?

"But," continued the argument, "a man degenerates
when he retires from active affairs." And then, instances
were pointed out as notable examples. "A year of retirement and he was through," was the picture given of one
retired man. "In two years, he was glad to come back,"
and so the examples ran on. "No big man ever retired

from active business and did great work afterwards," Bok
was told.

"No?" he answered. "Not even Cyrus W. Field or
Herbert Hoover?"

And all this time Edward Bok's failure to be entirely
Americanized was brought home to his consciousness.
After fifty years, he was still not an American! He had
deliberately planned, and then had carried out his plan,
to retire while he still had the mental and physical capacity to enjoy the fruits of his years of labor! For foreign to the American way of thinking it certainly was:
the protestations and arguments of his friends proved that
to him. After all, he was still Dutch; he had held on to
the lesson which his people had learned years ago; that the
people of other European countries had learned; that the
English had discovered: that the Great Adventure of Life
was something more than material work, and that the time
to go is while the going is good!

For it cannot be denied that the pathetic picture we so
often see is found in American business life more frequently
than in that of any other land: men unable to let go—not
only for their own good, but to give the younger men behind them an opportunity. Not that a man should stop
work, for man was born to work, and in work he should find
his greatest refreshment. But so often it does not occur
to the man in a pivotal position to question the possibility
that at sixty or seventy he can keep steadily in touch with
a generation whose ideas are controlled by men twenty
years younger. Unconsciously he hangs on beyond his
greatest usefulness and efficiency: he convinces himself
that he is indispensable to his business, while, in scores of
cases, the business would be distinctly benefited by his
retirement and the consequent coming to the front of the
younger blood.

Such a man in a position of importance seems often not to see that he has it within his power to advance the fortunes of younger men by stepping out when he has served his time, while by refusing to let go he often works dire injustice and even disaster to his younger associates.

The sad fact is that in all too many instances the average American business man is actually afraid to let go because he realizes that out of business he should not know what to do. For years he has so excluded all other interests that at fifty or sixty or seventy he finds himself a slave to his business, with positively no inner resources. Retirement from the one thing he does know would naturally leave such a man useless to himself and his family, and his community: worse than useless, as a matter of fact, for he would become a burden to himself, a nuisance to his family, and, when he would begin to write "letters" to the newspapers, a bore to the community.

It is significant that a European or English business man rarely reaches middle age devoid of acquaintance with other matters; he always lets the breezes from other worlds of thought blow through his ideas, with the result that when he is ready to retire from business he has other interests to fall back upon. Fortunately it is becoming less uncommon for American men to retire from business and devote themselves to other pursuits; and their number will undoubtedly increase as time goes on, and we learn the lessons of life with a richer background. But one cannot help feeling regretful that the custom is not growing more rapidly.

A man must unquestionably prepare years ahead for his retirement, not alone financially, but mentally as well. Bok noticed as a curious fact that nearly every business man who told him he had made a mistake in his retirement, and that the proper life for a man is to stick to the game

and see it through—"hold her nozzle agin the bank" as
Jim Bludso would say—was a man with no resources outside his business.   Naturally, a retirement is a mistake in
the eyes of such a man; but oh, the pathos of such a position: that in a world of so much interest, in an age so fas-
cinatingly full of things worth doing, a man should have
allowed himself to become a slave to his business, and
should imagine no other man happy without the same
claims!

It is this lesson that the American business man has
still to learn: that no man can be wholly efficient in his life,
that he is not living a four-squared existence, if he con-
centrates every waking thought on his material affairs.
He has still to learn that man cannot live by bread alone.
The making of money, the accumulation of material power,
is not all there is to living.   Life is something more than
these, and the man who misses this truth misses the greatest joy and satisfaction that can come into his life—service for others.

Some men argue that they can give this service and be
in business, too.   But service with such men generally
means drawing a check for some worthy cause, and nothing
more.   Edward Bok never belittled the giving of contributions—he solicited too much money himself for the causes
in which he was interested—but it is a poor nature that can
satisfy itself that it is serving humanity by merely signing
checks.   There is no form of service more comfortable or
so cheap.   Real service, however, demands that a man
give himself with his check.   And that the average man
cannot do if he remains in affairs.

Particularly true is this to-day, when every problem
of business is so engrossing, demanding a man's full time
and thought.   It is the rare man who can devote himself

to business and be fresh for the service of others afterward. No man can, with efficiency, serve two masters so exacting as are these. Besides, if his business has seemed important enough to demand his entire attention, are not the great uplift questions equally worth his exclusive thought? Are they easier of solution than the material problems?

A man can live a life full-square only when he divides it into three periods:

First: that of education, acquiring the fullest and best within his reach and power;

Second: that of achievement: achieving for himself and his family, and discharging the first duty of any man, that in case of his incapacity those who are closest to him are provided for. But such provision does not mean an accumulation that becomes to those he leaves behind him an embarrassment rather than a protection. To prevent this, the next period confronts him:

Third: Service for others. That is the acid test where many a man falls short: to know when he has enough, and to be willing not only to let well enough alone, but to give a helping hand to the other fellow; to recognize, in a practical way, that we are our brother's keeper; that a brotherhood of man does exist outside after-dinner speeches. Too many men make the mistake, when they reach the point of enough, of going on pursuing the same old game: accumulating more money, grasping for more power until either a nervous breakdown overtakes them and a sad incapacity results, or they drop "in the harness," which is, of course, only calling an early grave by another name. They cannot seem to get the truth into their heads that as they have been helped by others so should they now help others: as their means have come from the public, so now they owe something in turn to that public.

No man has a right to leave the world no better than he found it. He must add something to it: either he must make its people better and happier, or he must make the face of the world fairer to look at. And the one really means the other.

"Idealism," immediately say some. Of course, it is. But what is the matter with idealism? What really is idealism? Do one-tenth of those who use the phrase so glibly know its true meaning, the part it has played in the world? The worthy interpretation of an ideal is that it embodies an idea—a conception of the imagination. All ideas are at first ideals. They must be. The producer brings forth an idea, but some dreamer has dreamed it before him either in whole or in part.

Where would the human race be were it not for the ideals of men? It is idealists, in a large sense, that this old world needs to-day. Its soil is sadly in need of new seed. Washington, in his day, was decried as an idealist. So was Jefferson. It was commonly remarked of Lincoln that he was a "rank idealist." Morse, Watt, Marconi, Edison—all were, at first, adjudged idealists. We say of the League of Nations that it is ideal, and we use the term in a derogatory sense. But that was exactly what was said of the Constitution of the United States. "Insanely ideal" was the term used of it.

The idealist, particularly to-day when there is so great need of him, is not to be scoffed at. It is through him and only through him that the world will see a new and clear vision of what is right. It is he who has the power of going out of himself—that self in which too many are nowadays so deeply imbedded; it is he who, in seeking the ideal, will, through his own clearer perception or that of others, transform the ideal into the real. "Where there is no vision, the people perish."

It was his remark that he retired because he wanted
"to play" that Edward Bok's friends most completely
misunderstood. "Play" in their minds meant tennis,
golf, horseback, polo, travel, etc.—(curious that scarcely
one mentioned reading!). It so happens that no one en-
joys some of these play-forms more than Bok; but "God
forbid," he said, "that I should spend the rest of my days
in a bunker or in the saddle. In moderation," he added,
"yes; most decidedly." But the phrase of "play" meant
more to him than all this. Play is diversion: exertion of
the mind as well as of the body. There is such a thing as
mental play as well as physical play. We ask of play that
it shall rest, refresh, exhilarate. Is there any form of mental activity that secures all these ends so thoroughly and
so directly as doing something that a man really likes to
do, doing it with all his heart, all the time conscious that
he is helping to make the world better for some one else?

A man's "play" can take many forms. If his life has
been barren of books or travel, let him read or see the
world. But he reaches his high estate by either of these
roads only when he reads or travels to enrich himself in
order to give out what he gets to enrich the lives of others.
He owes it to himself to get his own refreshment, his own
pleasure, but he need not make that pure self-indulgence.

Other men, more active in body and mind, feel drawn
to the modern arena of the great questions that puzzle.
It matters not in which direction a man goes in these matters any more than the length of a step matters so much
as does the direction in which the step is taken. He should
seek those questions which engross his deepest interest,
whether literary, musical, artistic, civic, economic, or what
not.

Our cities, towns, communities of all sizes and kinds,
urban and rural, cry out for men to solve their problems.

There is room and to spare for the man of any bent. The old Romans looked forward, on coming to the age of retirement, which was definitely fixed by rule, to a rural life, when they hied themselves to a little home in the country, had open house for their friends, and "kept bees." While bee-keeping is unquestionably interesting, there are today other and more vital occupations awaiting the retired American.

The main thing is to secure that freedom of movement that lets a man go where he will and do what he thinks he can do best, and prove to himself and to others that the acquirement of the dollar is not all there is to life. No man can realize, until on awakening some morning he feels the exhilaration, the sense of freedom that comes from knowing he can choose his own doings and control his own goings. Time is of more value than money, and it is that which the man who retires feels that he possesses. Hamilton Mabie once said, after his retirement from an active editorial position: "I am so happy that the time has come when I elect what I shall do," which is true; but then he added: "I have rubbed out the word 'must' from my vocabulary," which was not true. No man ever reaches that point. Duty of some sort confronts a man in business or out of business, and duty spells "must." But there is less "must" in the vocabulary of the retired man; and it is this lessened quantity that gives the tang of joy to the new day.

It is a wonderful inner personal satisfaction to reach the point when a man can say: "I have enough." His soul and character are refreshed by it: he is made over by it. He begins a new life! he gets a sense of a new joy; he feels, for the first time, what a priceless possession is that thing that he never knew before, freedom. And if he seeks that freedom at the right time, when he is at the summit of his years and powers and at the most opportune moment in his affairs, he has that supreme satisfaction denied to so many men, the opposite of which comes home with such cruel force to them: that they have overstayed their time: they have worn out their welcome.

There is no satisfaction that so thoroughly satisfies as that of going while the going is good.

Still——

The friends of Edward Bok may be right when they said he made a mistake in his retirement.

However——

As Mr. Dooley says: "It's a good thing, sometimes, to have people size ye up wrong, Hinnessey: it's whin they've got ye'er measure ye're in danger."

Edward Bok's friends have failed to get his measure, —yet!

They still have to learn what he has learned and is learning every day: "the joy," as Charles Lamb so aptly put it upon his retirement, "of walking about and around instead of to and fro."

————

The question now naturally arises, having read this record thus far: To what extent, with his unusual opportunities of fifty years, has the Americanization of Edward Bok gone? How far is he, to-day, an American? These questions, so direct and personal in their nature, are perhaps best answered in a way more direct and personal than the method thus far adopted in this chronicle. We will, therefore, let Edward Bok answer these questions for himself, in closing this record of his Americanization.

CHAPTER XXI

When I came to the United States as a lad of six, the most needful lesson for me, as a boy, was the necessity for thrift. I had been taught in my home across the sea that thrift was one of the fundamentals in a successful life. My family had come from a land (the Netherlands) noted for its thrift; but we had been in the United States only a few days before the realization came home strongly to my father and mother that they had brought their children to a land of waste.

Where the Dutchman saved, the American wasted. There was waste, and the most prodigal waste, on every hand. In every street-car and on every ferry-boat the floors and seats were littered with newspapers that had been read and thrown away or left behind. If I went to a grocery store to buy a peck of potatoes, and a potato rolled off the heaping measure, the groceryman, instead of picking it up, kicked it into the gutter for the wheels of his wagon to run over. The butcher's waste filled my mother's soul with dismay. If I bought a scuttle of coal at the corner grocery, the coal that missed the scuttle, instead of being shovelled up and put back into the bin, was swept into the street. My young eyes quickly saw this; in the evening I gathered up the coal thus swept away, and during the course of a week I collected a scuttleful. The first time my mother saw the garbage pail of a family almost as poor as our own, with the wife and husband constantly complaining that they could not get along, she

194

could scarcely believe her eyes. A half pan of hominy of
the preceding day's breakfast lay in the pail next to a third
of a loaf of bread. In later years, when I saw, daily, a
scow loaded with the garbage of Brooklyn householders
being towed through New York harbor out to sea, it was
an easy calculation that what was thrown away in a week's
time from Brooklyn homes would feed the poor of the
Netherlands.

At school, I quickly learned that to "save money" was
to be "stingy"; as a young man, I soon found that the
American disliked the word "economy," and on every hand
as plenty grew spending grew. There was literally nothing
in American life to teach me thrift or economy; everything
to teach me to spend and to waste.

I saw men who had earned good salaries in their prime,
reach the years of incapacity as dependents. I saw families on every hand either living quite up to their means or
beyond them; rarely within them. The more a man earned,
the more he—or his wife—spent. I saw fathers and mothers
and their children dressed beyond their incomes. The proportion of families who ran into debt was far greater than
those who saved. When a panic came, the families "pulled
in"; when the panic was over, they "let out." But the
end of one year found them precisely where they were at
the close of the previous year, unless they were deeper in
debt.

It was in this atmosphere of prodigal expenditure and
culpable waste that I was to practise thrift: a fundamental
in life! And it is into this atmosphere that the foreign-
born comes now, with every inducement to spend and no
encouragement to save. For as it was in the days of my
boyhood, so it is to-day—only worse. One need only go
over the experiences of the past two years, to compare the

receipts of merchants who cater to the working-classes and the statements of savings-banks throughout the country, to read the story of how the foreign-born are learning the habit of criminal wastefulness as taught them by the American.

Is it any wonder, then, that in this, one of the essentials in life and in all success, America fell short with me, as it is continuing to fall short with every foreign-born who comes to its shores?

As a Dutch boy, one of the cardinal truths taught me was that whatever was worth doing was worth doing well: that next to honesty come thoroughness as a factor in success. It was not enough that anything should be done: it was not done at all if it was not done well. I came to America to be taught exactly the opposite. The two infernal Americanisms "That's good enough" and "That will do" were early taught me, together with the maxim of quantity rather than quality.

It was not the boy at school who could write the words in his copy-book best who received the praise of the teacher; it was the boy who could write the largest number of words in a given time. The acid test in arithmetic was not the mastery of the method, but the number of minutes required to work out an example. If a boy abbreviated the month January to "Jan." and the word Company to "Co." he received a hundred per cent mark, as did the boy who spelled out the words and who could not make the teacher see that "Co." did not spell "Company."

As I grew into young manhood, and went into business, I found on every hand that quantity counted for more than quality. The emphasis was almost always placed on how much work one could do in a day, rather than upon how

well the work was done.   Thoroughness was at a discount
on every hand; production at a premium.   It made no
difference in what direction I went, the result was the
same: the cry was always for quantity, quantity!   And
into this atmosphere of almost utter disregard for quality
I brought my ideas of Dutch thoroughness and my conviction that doing well whatever I did was to count as a cardinal principle in life.

During my years of editorship, save in one or two conspicuous instances, I was never able to assign to an American writer, work which called for painstaking research.   In
every instance, the work came back to me either incorrect
in statement, or otherwise obviously lacking in careful
preparation.

One of the most successful departments I ever conducted in *The Ladies' Home Journal* called for infinite
reading and patient digging, with the actual results sometimes almost negligible.   I made a study of my associates
by turning the department over to one after another, and
always with the same result: absolute lack of a capacity
for patient research.   As one of my editors, typically
American, said to me: "It isn't worth all the trouble that
you put into it."   Yet no single department ever repaid
the searcher more for his pains.   Save for assistance derived from a single person, I had to do the work myself for
all the years that the department continued.   It was ap-
parently impossible for the American to work with sufficient patience and care to achieve a result.

We all have our pet notions as to the particular evil
which is "the curse of America," but I always think that
Theodore Roosevelt came closest to the real curse when
he classed it as a lack of thoroughness.

Here again, in one of the most important matters in

life, did America fall short with me; and, what is more important, she is falling short with every foreigner that comes to her shores.

In the matter of education, America fell far short in what should be the strongest of all her institutions: the public school. A more inadequate, incompetent method of teaching, as I look back over my seven years of attendance at three different public schools, it is difficult to conceive. If there is one thing that I, as a foreign-born child, should have been carefully taught, it is the English language. The individual effort to teach this, if effort there was, and I remember none, was negligible. It was left for my father to teach me, or for me to dig it out for myself. There was absolutely no indication on the part of teacher or principal of responsibility for seeing that a foreign-born boy should acquire the English language correctly. I was taught as if I were American-born, and, of course, I was left dangling in the air, with no conception of what I was trying to do.

My father worked with me evening after evening; I plunged my young mind deep into the bewildering confusions of the language—and no one realizes the confusions of the English language as does the foreign-born—and got what I could through these joint efforts. But I gained nothing from the much-vaunted public-school system which the United States had borrowed from my own country, and then had rendered incompetent—either by a sheer disregard for the thoroughness that makes the Dutch public schools the admiration of the world, or by too close a regard for politics.

Thus, in her most important institution to the foreign-born, America fell short. And while I am ready to believe that the public school may have increased in efficiency since that day, it is, indeed, a question for the American to ponder, just how far the system is efficient for the education of the child who comes to its school without a knowledge of the first word in the English language. Without a detailed knowledge of the subject, I know enough of conditions in the average public school to-day to warrant at least the suspicion that Americans would not be particularly proud of the system, and of what it gives for which annually they pay millions of dollars in taxes.

I am aware in making this statement that I shall be met with convincing instances of intelligent effort being made with the foreign-born children in special classes. No one has a higher respect for those efforts than I have—few, other than educators, know of them better than I do, since I did not make my five-year study of the American public school system for naught. But I am not referring to the exceptional instance here and there. I merely ask of the American, interested as he is or should be in the Americanization of the strangers within his gates, how far the public school system, as a whole, urban and rural, adapts itself, with any true efficiency, to the foreign-born child. I venture to color his opinion in no wise; I simply ask that he will inquire and ascertain for himself, as he should do if he is interested in the future welfare of his country and his institutions; for what happens in America in the years to come depends, in large measure, on what is happening to-day in the public schools of this country.

As a Dutch boy I was taught a wholesome respect for law and for authority. The fact was impressed upon me that laws of themselves were futile unless the people for whom they were made respected them, and obeyed them in spirit more even than in the letter. I came to America to feel, on every hand, that exactly the opposite was true. Laws were passed, but were not enforced; the spirit to enforce them was lacking in the people. There was little respect for the law; there was scarcely any for those appointed to enforce it.

The nearest that a boy gets to the law is through the policeman. In the Netherlands a boy is taught that a policeman is for the protection of life and property; that he is the natural friend of every boy and man who behaves himself. The Dutch boy and the policeman are, naturally, friendly in their relations. I came to America to be told that a policeman is a boy's natural enemy; that he is eager to arrest him if he can find the slightest reason for doing so. A policeman, I was informed, was a being to hold in fear, not in respect. He was to be avoided, not to be made friends with. The result was that, as did all boys, I came to regard the policeman on our beat as a distinct enemy. His presence meant that we should "stiffen up"; his disappearance was the signal for us to "let loose."

So long as one was not caught, it did not matter. I heard mothers tell their little children that if they did not behave themselves, the policeman would put them into a bag and carry them off, or cut their ears off. Of course, the policeman became to them an object of terror; the law he represented, a cruel thing that stood for punishment. Not a note of respect did I ever hear for the law in my boyhood days. A law was something to be broken, to be evaded, to call down upon others as a source of punishment, but never to be regarded in the light of a safeguard.

And as I grew into manhood, the newspapers rang on every side with disrespect for those in authority. Under the special dispensation of the liberty of the press, which was construed into the license of the press, no man was too high to escape editorial vituperation if his politics did not happen to suit the management, or if his action ran counter to what the proprietors believed it should be. It was not criticism of his acts, it was personal attack upon the official; whether supervisor, mayor, governor, or president, it mattered not.

It is a very unfortunate impression that this American lack of respect for those in authority makes upon the foreign-born mind. It is difficult for the foreigner to square up the arrest and deportation of a man who, through an incendiary address, seeks to overthrow governmental authority, with the ignoring of an expression of exactly the same sentiments by the editor of his next morning's newspaper. In other words, the man who writes is immune, but the man who reads, imbibes, and translates the editor's words into action is immediately marked as a culprit, and America will not harbor him. But why harbor the original cause? Is the man who speaks with type less dangerous than he who speaks with his mouth or with a bomb?

At the most vital part of my life, when I was to become an American citizen and exercise the right of suffrage, America fell entirely short. It reached out not even the suggestion of a hand.

When the Presidential Conventions had been held in the year I reached my legal majority, and I knew I could vote, I endeavored to find out whether, being foreign-born, I was entitled to the suffrage. No one could tell me; and not until I had visited six different municipal departments, being referred from one to another, was it explained that, through my father's naturalization, I became, automatically, as his son, an American citizen. I decided to read up on the platforms of the Republican and Democratic parties, but I could not secure copies anywhere, although a week had passed since they had been adopted in convention.

I was told the newspapers had printed them. It occurred to me there must be many others besides myself who were anxious to secure the platforms of the two parties in some more convenient form. With the eye of necessity ever upon a chance to earn an honest penny, I went to a newspaper office, cut out from its files the two platforms, had them printed in a small pocket edition, sold one edition to the American News Company and another to the News Company controlling the Elevated Railroad bookstands in New York City, where they sold at ten cents each. So great was the demand which I had only partially guessed, that within three weeks I had sold such huge editions of the little books that I had cleared over a thousand dollars.

But it seemed to me strange that it should depend on a foreign-born American to supply an eager public with what should have been supplied through the agency of the political parties or through some educational source.

I now tried to find out what a vote actually meant. It must be recalled that I was only twenty-one years old, with scant education, and with no civic agency offering me the information I was seeking. I went to the headquarters of each of the political parties and put my query. I was regarded with puzzled looks.

"What does it mean to vote?" asked one chairman. "Why, on Election Day you go up to the ballot-box and put your ballot in, and that's all there is to it."

But I knew very well that that was not all there was

It was not to me; is it to him?

One fundamental trouble with the present desire for Americanization is that the American is anxious to Americanize two classes—if he is a reformer, the foreign-born; if he is an employer, his employees. It never occurs to him that he himself may be in need of Americanization. He seems to take it for granted that because he is American-born, he is an American in spirit and has a right understanding of American ideals. But that, by no means, always follows. There are thousands of the American-born who need Americanization just as much as do the foreign-born. There are hundreds of American employers who know far less of American ideals than do some of their employees. In fact, there are those actually engaged to-day in the work of Americanization, men at the top of the movement, who sadly need a better conception of true Americanism.

An excellent illustration of this came to my knowledge when I attended a large Americanization Conference in Washington. One of the principal speakers was an educator of high standing and considerable influence in one of the most important sections of the United States. In a speech setting forth his ideas of Americanization, he dwelt with much emphasis and at considerable length upon instilling into the mind of the foreign-born the highest respect for American institutions.

After the Conference he asked me whether he could see me that afternoon at my hotel; he wanted to talk about contributing to the magazine. When he came, before approaching the object of his talk, he launched out on a tirade against the President of the United States; the weakness of the Cabinet, the inefficiency of the Congress, and the stupidity of the Senate. If words could have killed,

to it, and was determined to find out the significance
the franchise. I met with dense ignorance on every han
I went to the Brooklyn Library, and was frankly told by t
librarian that he did not know of a book that would t
me what I wanted to know. This was in 1884.

As the campaign increased in intensity, I found myse
a desired person in the eyes of the local campaign managers
but not one of them could tell me the significance an
meaning of the privilege I was for the first time to exercise

Finally, I spent an evening with Seth Low, and, o
course, got the desired information.

But fancy the quest I had been compelled to make to
acquire the simple information that should have been
placed in my hands or made readily accessible to me. And
how many foreign-born would take equal pains to ascertain what I was determined to find out?

Surely America fell short here at the moment most
sacred to me: that of my first vote!

Is it any easier to-day for the foreign citizen to acquire
this information when he approaches his first vote? I
wonder! Not that I do not believe there are agencies for
this purpose. You know there are, and so do I. But how
about the foreign-born? Does he know it? Is it not perhaps like the owner of the bulldog who assured the friend
calling on him that it never attacked friends of the family?
"Yes," said the friend, "that's all right. You know and I
know that I am a friend of the family; but does the dog
know?"

Is it to-day made known to the foreign-born, about to
exercise his privilege of suffrage for the first time, where
he can be told what that privilege means: is the means to
know made readily accessible to him: is it, in fact, as i.
should be, brought to him?

there would have not remained a single living member of the Administration at Washington.

After fifteen minutes of this, I reminded him of his speech and the emphasis which he had placed upon the necessity of inculcating in the foreign-born respect for American institutions.

Yet this man was a power in his community, a strong influence upon others; he believed he could Americanize others, when he himself, according to his own statements, lacked the fundamental principle of Americanization. What is true of this man is, in lesser or greater degree, true of hundreds of others. Their Americanization consists of lip-service; the real spirit, the only factor which counts in the successful teaching of any doctrine, is absolutely missing. We certainly cannot teach anything approaching a true Americanism until we ourselves feel and believe and practise in our own lives what we are teaching to others. No law, no lip-service, no effort, however well-intentioned, will amount to anything worth while in inculcating the true American spirit in our foreign-born citizens until we are sure that the American spirit is understood by ourselves and is warp and woof of our own being.

To the American, part and parcel of his country, these particulars in which his country falls short with the foreign-born are, perhaps, not so evident; they may even seem not so very important. But to the foreign-born they seem distinct lacks; they loom large; they form serious handicaps which, in many cases, are never surmounted; they are a menace to that Americanization which is, to-day, more than ever our fondest dream, and which we now realize more keenly than before is our most vital need.

It is for this reason that I have put them down here as

a concrete instance of where and how America fell short
in my own Americanization, and, what is far more serious
to me, where she is falling short in her Americanization of
thousands of other foreign-born.

"Yet you succeeded," it will be argued.

That may be; but you, on the other hand, must admit
that I did not succeed by reason of these shortcomings: it
was in spite of them, by overcoming them—a result that
all might not achieve.

CHAPTER XXII

WHAT I OWE TO AMERICA

Whatever shortcomings I may have found during my fifty-year period of Americanization; however America may have failed to help my transition from a foreigner into an American, I owe to her the most priceless gift that any nation can offer, and that is opportunity.

As the world stands to-day, no nation offers opportunity in the degree that America does to the foreign-born. Russia may, in the future, as I like to believe she will, prove a second United States of America in this respect. She has the same limitless area; her people the same potentialities. But, as things are to-day, the United States offers, as does no other nation, a limitless opportunity: here a man can go as far as his abilities will carry him. It may be that the foreign-born, as in my own case, must hold on to some of the ideals and ideas of the land of his birth; it may be that he must develop and mould his character by overcoming the habits resulting from national shortcomings. But into the best that the foreign-born can retain, America can graft such a wealth of inspiration, so high a national idealism, so great an opportunity for the highest endeavor, as to make him the fortunate man of the earth to-day.

He can go where he will; no traditions hamper him; no limitations are set except those within himself. The larger the area he chooses in which to work, the larger the vision he demonstrates, the more eager the people are to give support to his undertakings if they are convinced that he has their best welfare as his goal. There is no public confidence equal to that of the American public, once it is obtained. It is fickle, of course, as are all publics, but fickle only toward the man who cannot maintain an achieved success.

A man in America cannot complacently lean back upon victories won, as he can in the older European countries, and depend upon the glamour of the past to sustain him or the momentum of success to carry him. Probably the most alert public in the world, it requires of its leaders that they be alert. Its appetite for variety is insatiable, but its appreciation, when given, is full-handed and whole-hearted. The American public never holds back from the man to whom it gives; it never bestows in a niggardly way; it gives all or nothing.

What is not generally understood of the American people is their wonderful idealism. Nothing so completely surprises the foreign-born as the discovery of this trait in the American character. The impression is current in European countries—perhaps less generally since the war —that America is given over solely to a worship of the American dollar. While between nations as between individuals, comparisons are valueless, it may not be amiss to say, from personal knowledge, that the Dutch worship the gulden infinitely more than do the Americans the dollar.

I do not claim that the American is always conscious of this idealism; often he is not. But let a great convulsion touching moral questions occur, and the result always shows how close to the surface is his idealism. And the fact that so frequently he puts over it a thick veneer of materialism does not affect its quality. The truest approach, the only approach in fact, to the American character is, as Viscount Bryce has so well said, through its idealism.

It is this quality which gives the truest inspiration to the foreign-born in his endeavor to serve the people of his adopted country. He is mentally sluggish, indeed, who does not discover that America will make good with him if he makes good with her.

But he must play fair. It is essentially the straight game that the true American plays, and he insists that you shall play it too. Evidence there is, of course, to the contrary in American life, experiences that seem to give ground for the belief that the man succeeds who is not scrupulous in playing his cards. But never is this true in the long run. Sooner or later—sometimes, unfortunately, later than sooner—the public discovers the trickery. In no other country in the world is the moral conception so clear and true as in America, and no people will give a larger and more permanent reward to the man whose effort for that public has its roots in honor and truth.

"The sky is the limit" to the foreign-born who comes to America endowed with honest endeavor, ceaseless industry, and the ability to carry through. In any honest endeavor, the way is wide open to the will to succeed. Every path beckons, every vista invites, every talent is called forth, and every efficient effort finds its due reward. In no land is the way so clear and so free.

How good an American has the process of Americanization made me? That I cannot say. Who *can* say that of himself? But when I look around me at the American-born I have come to know as my close friends, I wonder whether, after all, the foreign-born does not make in some sense a better American—whether he is not able to get a truer perspective; whether his is not the deeper desire to see America greater; whether he is not less content to let its faulty institutions be as they are; whether in seeing faults more clearly he does not make a more decided effort to have America reach those ideals or those fundamentals of his own land which he feels are in his nature, and the best of which he is anxious to graft into the character of his adopted land?

It is naturally with a feeling of deep satisfaction that I remember two Presidents of the United States considered me a sufficiently typical American to wish to send me to my native land as the accredited minister of my adopted country. And yet when I analyze the reasons for my choice in both these instances, I derive a deeper satisfaction from the fact that my strong desire to work in America for America led me to ask to be permitted to remain here.

It is this strong impulse that my Americanization has made the driving power of my life. And I ask no greater privilege than to be allowed to live to see my potential America become actual: the America that I like to think of as the America of Abraham Lincoln and of Theodore Roosevelt—not faultless, but less faulty. It is a part in trying to shape that America, and an opportunity to work in that America when it comes, that I ask in return for what I owe to her. A greater privilege no man could have.

EDWARD WILLIAM BOK

BIOGRAPHICAL DATA

1863: October 9: Born at Helder, Netherlands.

1870: September 20: Arrived in the United States.

1870: Entered public schools of Brooklyn, New York.

1873: Obtained first position in Frost's Bakery, Smith Street, Brooklyn, at 50 cents per week.

1876: August 7: Entered employ of the Western Union Telegraph Company as office-boy.

1882: Entered employ of Henry Holt & Company as stenographer.

1884: Entered employ of Charles Scribner's Sons as stenographer.

1884: Became editor of *The Brooklyn Magazine*.

1886: Founded the Bok Syndicate Press.

1887: Published Henry Ward Beecher Memorial (privately printed).

1889: October 20: Became editor of *The Ladies' Home Journal*.

1890: Published *Successward :* Doubleday, McClure & Company.

1894: Published *Before He Is Twenty :* Fleming H. Revell Company.

1896: October 22: Married Mary Louise Curtis.

1897: September 7: Son born: William Curtis Bok.

1900: Published *The Young Man in Business:* L. C. Page & Company.

1905: January 25: Son born: Cary William Bok.

1906: Published *Her Brother's Letters* (Anonymous): Moffat, Yard & Company.

1907: Degree of LL.D. of Order of Augustinian Fathers conferred by order of Pope Pius X., by the Most Reverend Diomede Falconio, D.D., Apostolic Delegate to the United States, at Villanova College.

1910: Degree of LL.D. conferred, in absentia, by Hope College, Holland, Michigan (the only Dutch college in the United States).

1911: Founded, with others, The Child Federation of Philadelphia.

1912: Published *The Edward Bok Books of Self-Knowledge;* five volumes: Fleming H. Revell Company.

1913: Founded, with others, The Merion Civic Association, at Merion, Pennsylvania.

1915: Published *Why I Believe in Poverty:* Houghton, Mifflin Company.

1916: Published poem, *God's Hand,* set to music by Josef Hofmann: Schirmer & Company.

1917: Vice-president Philadelphia Belgian Relief Commission.

1917: Member of National Y. M. C. A. War Work Council.

1917: State chairman for Pennsylvania of Y. M. C. A. War Work Council.

1918: Member of Executive Committee and chairman of Publicity Committee, Philadelphia War Chest.

1918: Chairman of Philadelphia Y. M. C. A. Recruiting Committee.

1918: State chairman for Pennsylvania of United War Work Campaign.

1918: August–November: visited the battle-fronts in France as guest of the British Government.

1919: September 22: Relinquished editorship of *The Ladies' Home Journal,* completing thirty years of service.

1920: September 20: Upon the 50th anniversary of arrival in the United States, published *The Americanization of Edward Bok.*

1921: May 30: Awarded the one thousand dollar Joseph Pulitzer Prize for *The Americanization of Edward Bok.*

THE EXPRESSION OF A PERSONAL PLEASURE

I cannot close this record of a boy's development without an attempt to suggest the sense of deep personal pleasure which I feel that the imprint on the title-page of this book should be that of the publishing house which, thirty-six years ago, I entered as stenographer. It was there I received my start; it was there I laid the foundation of that future career then so hidden from me. The happiest days of my young manhood were spent in the employ of this house; I there began friendships which have grown closer with each passing year. And one of my deepest sources of satisfaction is, that during all the thirty-one years which have followed my resignation from the Scribner house, it has been my good fortune to hold the friendship, and, as I have been led to believe, the respect of my former employers. That they should now be my publishers demonstrates, in a striking manner, the curious turning of the wheel of time, and gives me a sense of gratification difficult of expression.

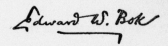

INDEX

215